LEAVES FROM THREE ANCIENT QURÂNS

POSSIBLY PRE-'OTHMÂNIC

LEAVES FROM THREE ANCIENT QURÂNS POSSIBLY PRE-'OTHMÂNIC

with a list of their Variants

Edited by

REV. ALPHONSE MINGANA, D.D.

Late Professor of Semitic Languages and Literature in the Syro-Chaldaean Seminary at Mosul;

and

AGNES SMITH LEWIS

Hon. D.D. (Heidelberg); LL.D. (St Andrews); Litt.D. (Dublin); Ph.D. (Halle-Wittenberg)

Cambridge:
at the University Press
1914

CAMBRIDGE
UNIVERSITY PRESS

University Printing House, Cambridge CB2 8BS, United Kingdom

Cambridge University Press is part of the University of Cambridge.

It furthers the University's mission by disseminating knowledge in the pursuit of education, learning and research at the highest international levels of excellence.

www.cambridge.org
Information on this title: www.cambridge.org/9781107438040

First published 1914
First paperback edition 2014

A catalogue record for this publication is available from the British Library

ISBN 978-1-107-43804-0 Paperback

PREFACE

THE manuscript from which these leaves are taken was bought by me at Suez from a commercial antiquary on his travels in 1895. It is a palimpsest, the upper script being a series of closely-written Homilies in Arabic by early Christian Fathers, such as Theodosius, Chrysostom and Mar Jacob. This was pronounced by Dr Cowley, of Oxford, and Mr Ellis, who was then at the British Museum, to be written in a style which is assigned to the very end of the ninth century, or to the beginning of the tenth one, and which was in vogue for a very short time.

Eighty-four leaves of the under script contain a text of the *Protevangelium Jacobi* and the *Transitus Mariae* in two columns of Estrangelo Syriac. I brought this up with a re-agent, hydro-sulphide of ammonia, and published it in 1902 as No. XI *Studia Sinaitica*. It was not quite appropriate for that series; for I have no reason to think that it was ever at Sinai; but at that time I had no intention of returning to St Catherine's Convent; and *Horae Semiticae* had not then been thought of.

Among the Syriac quires were six Arabic ones; while several miscellaneous leaves, in both languages, were scattered through the same volume, as is the manner of palimpsest MSS. which were written when vellum was very scarce. The vellum of the *Protevangelium* and the *Transitus* did not suffice for the ninth century scribe, for he pressed into his service one leaf of the Greek Septuagint, containing a text from Gen. xli, and several leaves that have been twice palimpsested with texts from the Syriac Old Testament; that is to say, there are three very good writings, crossing each other, on all these pages. I contented myself with deciphering only one of the under scripts, and thus obtained portions of Exodus and Isaiah, of which more may yet be heard. The under script of another leaf which I published in No. XI was called by me a hymn. My friend Dr Mingana considers it rather to be part of a Commentary.

There are other curious things in it, the decipherment of which has baffled my own skill, and also that of some very capable Arabists. I am in the habit of exhibiting one leaf which has five different scripts on it, including the rough label of one of its commercial owners; three scripts, each of them covering the whole page; and some tiny lines, in a different hand, on the margin. Amongst this curious medley are what I took to be 44 leaves of Kūfic Arabic, in six quires. As it lies crossways to the very clear ninth century upper script, there are naturally four lines at least running along the margins on each page, that are more easily read than the remainder. A little patient study revealed to me the fact that they were from the Qurân. I contented myself with verifying to which Sūrah and which verse they belong; and with copying the lines at the top and bottom of each half-page. I found no less than 42 words which I thought were wrongly spelt, such as اوليك for اولايك. What is generally called the Noun Agent of verbs in the first form both in the singular and in the plural, is written without the usual Alif after the first radical letter, excepting where an ambiguity would otherwise ensue.

If the reader wishes to understand why I did not transcribe more of the text, he has only to glance at the tangle of cross-writings in my illustrations, and remember that while I am familiar with the Naskhi script of Arabic, and am not quite a stranger to Kūfic, this script is neither the one nor the other, but a kind of writing which, *me judice*, is very seldom seen. I was also prepossessed by the belief that all copies of the Qurân are in duty bound to be exactly alike. The same causes must have influenced all my Arabist friends, and all Oriental readers of No. XI *Studia Sinaitica*; for no suggestion has ever been made to me, during the eleven years that have elapsed since that book was published, that the subject might possibly repay further investigation.

It was on Nov. 27, 1913, when Dr Mingana spent two days in our house, that the idea occurred to me of shewing him my book entitled *Apocrypha Syriaca*, i.e. No. XI. As he turned its pages I was suddenly startled by the question, "What are you doing with *sics* in the Qurân?" "Because they are there," I replied, "and I can shew you where I got them." On comparing the MS. with my printed lines, however, Dr Mingana said that forty-one of the words to which I had put a *sic* are only archaic spellings; but that one in Sūrah 7 can have a distinct difference of meaning; it is الله وكلمته "God and His Word," instead of الله وكلماته "God and His Words" as in the Authorized text.

I was only too glad to find a learned Assyrian scholar, whose eyes are much younger and sharper than mine, and whose native language is Arabic, willing to undertake so difficult a task as the decipherment of my pages. The result has greatly surprised me. Few can read the list of variants given on pp. xxxvii—xli without perceiving that many of them fit better into their context, and are more likely to have been dictated by the Prophet and written by Zaid ibn Thâbit than those which have been doing duty for 1300 years instead of them.

As Dr Mingana's transcription has been made in our house, each variant, as he found it, was verified at once by me, and most of them also by my sister, Dr Margaret Dunlop Gibson. Not till we were both satisfied did it go into his transcript.

We think that these leaves are pre-'Othmânic for this reason. Muḥammad, when he believed that he was receiving supernatural revelations, employed Zaid ibn Thâbit to write them down for him, and this Zaid did, on potsherds, palm-leaves, strips of vellum, or whatever came handy. No doubt copies of the different Sūrahs were afterwards made by Zaid himself, when sufficient writing material had been obtained. It is not surprising if these contained some mistakes in spelling; especially as the rules of Arabic grammar were not then fixed. But after Muḥammad's death, Abu Bekr and 'Othmân had all these writings properly copied out and arranged in the form with which we have become familiar. In this work, be it noted, they had the help of Zaid. 'Othmân then ordered all the earlier copies to be destroyed; and the text of the Qurân, as it now stands, obtained a position of unique and unchallenged authority over the Moslem world. We therefore cannot imagine anyone attempting the useless task of writing out a text like ours, after the time of 'Othmân.

Putting all the facts together, as they are known to ourselves, or as they have been handed down to us by a credible tradition, we think that these vellum leaves, now happily my property, were amongst those whose destruction was ordered by 'Othmân and was incumbent on all true believers in Islâm. There are two ways of destroying manuscripts. The most effectual one is by burning; but in those early days vellum was scarce—

especially in the desert—the papyrus reed had disappeared, having been utterly uprooted for the needs of literary folk; and paper was unknown, except in China. The owner of Qurâns which had been prematurely written, was surely justified in thinking that if he got rid of their text, by means of pumice-stone or otherwise, the attenuated vellum might remain, and its price might help to equip himself for a *jehâd*. By sale therefore, or barter, this one passed into the hands of Christian monks; and then, towards the end of the ninth century, it was written clearly over with choice extracts from the Fathers of the Church; the pages being folded double, and some of them being clipped to a smaller size to make them fit in with those of the *Transitus Mariae*. I think it very probable that the writer of the second script did not suspect that any of the vellum he used had an earlier text on it. Dr Rendel Harris, who was for several years Lecturer in Palaeography to the University of Cambridge, and who may be regarded as an expert in palimpsests, shares this opinion. There is no record, so far as I know, of the history of such documents; for in most cases their owners would never notice how long a period had elapsed between the effacement of the first writing and its re-appearance.

The less the manuscript was exposed to the action of the air, the longer would be the time before this took place.

I have already given a description of the manuscript in No. XI *Studia Sinaitica*. The leaves of the Qurân are a very little smaller than those of the *Protevangelium*, i.e. nearly 20 centimetres by 12. But those of Qurân A were certainly larger, and have been cut down to the size of their neighbours by the ninth century scribe; Qurân A, called by me Qurân I, forms the two final quires of the volume, extending from folio 147 to folio 161; and being interrupted only by foll. 155 and 162, which are taken from another manuscript whose script, being very small, is practically buried under the text of Mar Jacob which forms the upper ninth century writing. The 31 leaves in four quires, which I called Qurân II, have been found by Dr Mingana to belong to two different MSS., and are therefore re-named B and C.

To those who have never handled a palimpsest it may be right to mention that I have followed the arrangement of the later script in numbering the pages of the whole book; thus two pages of the later Christian Arabic script correspond to one only of the earlier

Qurân one; the original pages of the whole book having been folded double and turned sideways by the ninth century scribe. Therefore the Qurân pages always bear two numbers, such as 18 a and 15 b.

I could have read no page of the Syriac *Protevangelium* nor of anything else completely, if I had not begun by cutting the cords which held the book together, and smoothing out the pages. These binding cords have made numerous holes in the inner margins. Qurân A, as I must now call it, is written on much stronger vellum than B and C are; some pages of the latter are beginning to split and crumble. This is not wonderful, since it was thin to begin with; and more than a thousand years ago it was rubbed hard with pumice-stone for the purpose of completely obliterating every word of the Qurân text which had been impressed on it.

After publishing No. XI in 1902, my first care was to place the manuscript in the hands of expert binders, Messrs Eyre and Spottiswoode, whose workshops are now attached to the British Museum. The vellum leaves have been by them set within strong paper ones, and the more ragged leaves have been mended with strips of very fine transparent white gauze. This gauze has been somewhat of an impediment to Dr Mingana's work; yet without it some of the pages would not exist for him to decipher. Some of them have suffered so much from age and neglect that they have become undecipherable. In these cases we have indicated the missing text by a few rows of dots; but in places where only a word or two is undoubtedly there, although it is illegible, we have given the probable text from the standard Qurân; placing the borrowed words in square brackets, and adding a point of interrogation (?) where there is a doubt.

How did this manuscript come into my hands? And why should I have put it under the eyes of Dr Mingana, who is, of all men I know, the most competent to decipher it? I leave others to explain this. Some may attribute it to what the Moslems call "Kismet," which is not exactly the same as what the Christians regard as Providence.

And now I must be allowed to congratulate heartily my Moslem fellow countrymen on the gift which, by the hands of Dr Mingana, I now venture to offer them. The discovery of variants in our Jewish and Christian sacred books has been an untold blessing to our generation. If in Jerome's day the Roman Pontiff had been sufficiently powerful or sufficiently ill-advised to order the destruction of every copy of the New Testament except the Vulgate, we should have been in a position analogous to that of the present-day Moslems. Try to imagine what we should have done without Codd. Sinaiticus, Vaticanus, Bezae, etc., without the Old Latin, and without the Syriac Versions. We should have been doing penance for our sins, perhaps, without always truly repenting; and a powerful stimulus to the searching of the Scriptures would have been wanting. The existence of variants in Greek MSS. and in the Versions has been a means of waking us up; a thorough examination of the Bible text preceded and accompanied the Reformation of the sixteenth century; and accompanies also the present great activity of Christian Missionaries. Uneducated people do not generally wish to think; they therefore welcome the idea of verbal and even of literal inspiration. Educated people, on the contrary, find no subject more engrossing than the study and elucidation of God's truth; whether by means of natural science, of human history, or of the text of His Word. The last of these subjects helps to keep highly trained minds imbued with religious thought. And when the best intellects in any nation cease to be religious, indifference and apathy creep downward among the multitude, and are closely followed by superstition. I therefore venture to indulge the hope that a search beneath the writing of ancient MSS. in the libraries and museums of Europe may result in the discovery of more pre-'Othmânic portions of the Qurân, and that ours may prove to be only the first drops of a shower; an occurrence which has happened already, in my own experience, to the Hebrew text of Ben-Sira, of which the first leaf was identified by Dr S. Schechter.

The texts of the Qurân with which we have collated that of our fragments are those of the MSS. numbered Or. 1340 and Or. 1401 in the British Museum; the Qurân of Tippoo Sahib in the Cambridge University Library, one which belongs to Dr Mingana, and the printed text of Gustav Flügel. Our thanks are due to my dear sister, Dr Margaret D. Gibson, for help in revising proofs; and to the printers of the University Press, for their careful and accurate work.

AGNES SMITH LEWIS.

CASTLE-BRAE, CAMBRIDGE.

May, 1914.

INTRODUCTION

I

ABOUT 611 A.D. an illustrious member of the Arabic tribe of Ḳuraish heard, in the cave of Ḥira, a voice giving him the solemn message: "Cry thou in the name of thy Lord who created, created man from clots of blood." Sūratul-'Alaḳ (xcvi. 1–2[1]).

Whatever be the degree of credence that an impartial critic may bestow upon this tradition, held as an unshakable truth by more than two hundred and fifty millions of people, we must at least bear in mind that a tradition sanctioned during the long period of thirteen centuries should command a certain respect and trust.

The man who heard this secret voice was Muḥammad, and the result of the recital of the message that he received is Muḥammadanism, whose only foundation is the book entitled Al-Qur'ân, which originally means "recital" *par excellence.*

It is only during the last centuries that the Qurân has been studied scientifically, and the outcome of genuine researches on this subject induces us to face to-day the Islâmic book with a mental composure somewhat in contrast to the enthusiastic and often blind fascination which characterizes the Qurânic compositions of the Muḥammadan world. For this reason, we earnestly wish that the spirit of a higher criticism would soon be created among modern Moslem theologians, who, attracted by so many Christian theologians, commentators, and exegetes, will then give up the puerile servility in which they have lived and still live, and the low traditionalism of doctrine which tarnishes all the beauty of their writings.

---

[1] اقرا باسم ربك الذي خلق: خلق الانسان من علق. See a striking narration in the annalist *Ibn Hishâm*, p. 152, l. 9 sqq., who represents the Prophet as responding to this voice: "What shall I cry?" We cannot help thinking of the following words found in the prophet Isaiah (xl. 6): קול אמר קרא: ואמר מה אקרא: "The voice of (one) saying, *Cry*, and he said What shall I cry?" The verb قرا, קרא which is used in both texts in the same sense will establish a curious and hardly accidental coincidence.

Let us see what Muḥammad himself thinks of the inspired book by means of which he tried, if possible, to overthrow the Christian and the Jewish bulwarks, by sapping at their base, the foundations of all that the old Prophets and the Apostles handed down to their respective admirers:

"Say verily, were men and jinns assembled to produce the like of this Qurân they could not produce its like, though the one should help the other." (Sūrat Bani Isrâ'il, xvii. 90[1].)

"If they say, 'The Qurân is his own device' say, 'Then bring ten Sūrahs like it of your own devising; call whom ye can to your aid besides Allah.'" (Sūrat Hūd, xi. 16[2].)

"If ye be in doubt as to that which we have sent down to our servant, then produce a Sūrah like it." (Sūratul-Baqarah, ii. 21[3].)

"The Muḥammadan writers, in acknowledging the claims of the Qurân to be the direct utterance of the divinity, have made it impossible for any Moslem to criticise the work, and it became, on the contrary, the standard by which other literary compositions had to be judged. Grammarians, lexicographers, and rhetoricians, started with the presumption that the Qurân could not be wrong, and that all works only approached excellence in proportion as they more or less successfully imitated its style[4]."

Before we examine the truth of these assertions, we would wish to direct the attention of every reader of the Qurân to the following points: (1) The sources of the Qurân. (2) If we strip from its text the historical events and the circumstances in which it was written, it becomes an inexplicable composition. (3) How were the verses of the Qurân preserved from 612 to 632? (4) Who is the compiler of the standard text that we have to-day, and is this compilation authentic?

The first point is very easily treated, and since the Prophet could probably neither read nor write[5], the details which deal with the unity of God, and with the various forms of the eastern conceptions of religious obligations, viz. prayer, alms, fasting, etc. must have been inspired chiefly by oral information drawn from Christians, and specially from the strong Jewish colony of Mecca and the

---

1 قل لئن اجتمعت الانس والجن على ان ياتوا بمثل هذا القران لا ياتون بمثله ولو كان بعضهم لبعضهم ظهيرا

2 ام يقولون افتراه قل فاتوا بعشر سور مثله مفتريات وادعوا من استطعتم من دون الله

3 وان كنتم في ريب مما نزلنا على عبدنا فاتوا بسورة من مثله

4 Palmer, *Sacred Books of the East*, vol. VI. pp. 55, 71, etc.

5 The question whether Muḥammad could read and write is discussed but not decided by Nöldeke, *Geschichte des Qorâns*, p. 7 sqq.

neighbouring districts. Besides the masterly book of Nöldeke, the reader will find trustworthy information on this subject in Geiger's *Was hat Mahomet aus dem Judenthum aufgenommen?* (1833) for the Jewish element in the Qurân, and in W. St Clair Tisdall's *The original sources of the Qurân* (1905). Some good ideas may be found in Cl. Huart's *Une nouvelle source du Qorân* (1904). We have to draw attention to the following details:

Long before the time of the Prophet, the Ḳuraishites were mixed with the Christians, and about 485 A.D. a well-known Syrian writer, Narsai, the founder of the University of Nisibis, mentions the terrible raids that the forefathers of Muḥammad were wont to make in the district of Beith 'Arabayé, in Western Assyria: "The raid of the sons of Hagar was more cruel even than famine, and the blow that they gave was more sore than disease; the wound of the sons of Abram is like the venom of a serpent, and perhaps there is a remedy for the poison of reptiles, but not for theirs....Let us always blame the foul inclination of the sons of Hagar, and specially the people (the tribe) of Ḳuraish who are like animals[1]."

The distance between Arabia and the desert of Syria will not astonish our reader if he thinks of the semi-nomad life of every good Arab, when mounted on his swift mare. We read in *Synodicon Orientale*[2] that about 486 A.D. the famous Barṣauma of Nisibis was appointed with Ḳardagh Nakwergân, Roman *dux* and king of the Arabs, to settle the differences arising out of the rudimental delimitation of the Roman and Persian frontiers, in the East of Arabia. A letter from Barṣauma to Acacius, Catholicos of Seleucia, informs us that the Arabs called Ṭu'âites would not have permitted the inhabitants of the province of Beith 'Arabayé to live in peace through their continual raids. These Arabs, who are not to be confounded with Ṭayayés, Ṭay, and who molested so strangely the Western parts of the old Assyrian empire, were living in the sandy plains of the South-Western land of the Sassanides, and by their proximity to the country of the Meccan prophet they must have shaken more than once the primitive religious authorities of central Arabia. In the districts adjoining the country where Mecca is situated, several small kingdoms were almost half Christian, and a document of supreme value[3] proves that Ḥîra was already a bishopric in 410 A.D.

---

[1] A. Mingana, *Narsai Homiliae et Carmina*, 1905, vol. I. pp. 115–116 and 117 n. 1 in changing ܩܕ̈ܫܝܐ into ܩܪ̈ܫܝܐ as the MS. requires.

[2] *Recueil des actes synodaux de l'Église de Perse*, edit. Chabot, in "Notice et extraits des manuscrits," t. XXXVII. pp. 532, 534, 536 *et passim*.

[3] *Syn. Orient.* p. 275. Cf. on this question Duchesne, *Les Églises séparées*, pp. 337–352: "Les Missions Chrétiennes au Sud de l'empire romain, les Arabes."

In consideration of the meagre scientific attainments of the Prophet, the question of the sources of the Qurân has been keenly debated by the old Christian communities. The outcome of some of their thoughts brought forth the curious *History of Rabban Beḥîra.* The second part of this legend which tells of the interview of Muḥammad with this monk, and the epoch of whose composition may be the middle of the VIIIth century, is an irrefragable proof both of the ignorance of the Christian scholars of that time about the genuine sources of the Qurân, and of their conviction that it had a foreign origin. M. R. Gottheil, who printed this history in 1899[1], remarks that its first part, containing the encounter of Beḥîra with Išo'iahb, and its third part, exhibiting some apocalyptic visions on Islâm, may date from the XIth century, but its second part is much earlier. It would be interesting to know whether this second part has no historical value; but as this question is a digression from our subject, we content ourselves with a reference to it.

The internal criticism of the Qurân will easily shew this elementary evidence of a foreign source; but what we can by no means explain, are the wonderful anachronisms about the old Israelite history. The only possible way of accounting for these would be the distance which separated the moment of the inspiration of the verses from the moment when the Prophet received the oral communication. Who then will not be astonished to learn that in the Qurân, Miriam, the sister of Aaron, is confounded with the Virgin Mary? (Sūrat Ali-'Imrân, iii. 31 *et seq.*) and that Haman is given as minister of Pharaoh, instead of Ahasuerus? (Sūratul-Qaṣaṣ, xxviii. 38. Sūratul-Mu'men, xl. 38 *et passim.*) The ignorance, too, of the author of the Qurân about everything outside of Arabia and some parts of Syria makes the fertility of Egypt, where rain is never missed, for the simple reason that it is very seldom seen, depend on rain instead of on the inundation of the Nile[2]. (Sūrat Yūsuf, xii. 49.) Moreover, the greatest honour that the Israelite tradition bestows upon Esdras is found in *Sanhedrin*, xxi. 22, where we read that "'Ezra would have been fully worthy to give the law, if Moses had not been before him[3]"; but to state, as in Sūratut-Taubah, ix. 30, that the Jews believed that Esdras was the son of God, as the Christians thought of the Messiah, is a grave error hardly justifiable. All these historical mistakes receive another and not less topical support from the utter confusion which is made between Gideon and Saul in Sūratul-Baqarah, ii. 250. Such mistakes are indelible stains on the pages of the sacred book which is the

---

[1] *Zeitschr. für Assyriologie*, XII. pp. 189–242.

[2] ثم ياتي من بعد ذلك (that is in Egypt) عام فيه يغاث الناس وفيه يعصرون.

[3] Cf. a passage of Josephus (Ant. XI. 5) which tells his high repute (δόξα) with the people.

object of our study, and they are not wiped out by the following statement:

"We (Allah) relate unto thee a most excellent history, by revealing unto thee this Qurân, whereas thou wast before one of the negligent[1]." (Sūrat Yūsuf, xii. 3.) And again,

"I (Muḥammad) had no knowledge of the exalted princes when they disputed about the creation of man; it is revealed unto me only as a proof that I am a public preacher[2]." (Sūrat Ṣad, xxxviii. 67–70.)

If we try to read the Qurân from beginning to end in the order in which it has been circulated from the latter half of the VIIth century down to this day, we shall ascertain that it is the most incoherent of books, and the flagrant contradictions that we shall meet will astonish us. So in Sūratut-Taubah, we read, "Make war upon the people unto whom the book has been delivered, who... forbid not what Allah and His Apostle have forbidden, and who profess not the profession of the truth, until they pay tribute out of hand in an humble condition[3]." And again in Sūratul-Baqarah, ii. 189, it is said: "And fight against them till there be no more tumult, and the only worship be that of Allah[4]."

But in this same Sūratul-Baqarah, v. 257, it is said: "Let there be no compulsion in religion[5]"; and in Sūratul-'Ankabūt, xxix. 45: "And dispute ye not, except in kindliest sort with the people of the book[6]." (The Christians and the Jews, by allusion to the Torah and the Gospel, are called in the Qurân *the people of the book.*)

The Muḥammadan Commentators noticed these contradictions, and found that the best way to remove them was that of the historical method, and availing themselves of the oldest lives of the Prophet by Zuhri, Mūsa ibn 'Uqba, Abu Isḥâḳ, Madâ'ini, and the better-known books of Ibn Hishâm, Wâḳidi, and Ṭabari, they attempted to explain every verse by the circumstances in which it has been revealed, and they distributed the Sūrahs of the Qurân into two distinct groups: those which were written in Mecca from 612 A.D. to 622, and

---

[1] نحن نقص عليك احسن القصص بما اوحينا اليك هذا القرآن وان كنت من قبله لمن الغافلين

[2] ما كان لي من علم بالملا الاعلى اذ يختصمون. ان يوحى الي الا انما انا نذير مبين

[3] قاتلوا الذين لا ... يحرمون ما حرم الله ورسوله ولا يدينون دين الحق من الذين اوتوا الكتاب حتى يعطوا الجزية عن يد وهم صاغرون

[4] وقاتلوهم حتى لا تكون فتنة ويكون الدين لله

[5] لا اكراه في الدين

[6] ولا تجادلوا اهل الكتاب الا بالتي هي احسن

those which were revealed in Medîna, from 622 to 632. The youthful and timid essay of Muḥammadan theologians has been in the last few years considerably expanded by many critics; special mention must be made here of Nöldeke's *Geschichte des Qorâns* (1860), and E. Sell's *The historical development of the Qorân* (1905).

By this synchronal method, the Qurân becomes a historical book, and the most trustworthy source of information about the Prophet. The touchstone of veracity for any given detail of the life of Muḥammad told by the historians of the period of decadence would be to find if this detail has any sufficient ground in the Islâmic book. But, at any rate, if by this criticism, the chronological order is saved, the versatility of mind of the Prophet can by no means be excused, since, under the pressure of necessity, he cruelly contradicted sometimes what he had stated before. Can then the following verse inspired in Mecca excuse some flagrant contradictions of the Qurân?:

"And we have not sent an apostle or prophet before thee, among whose desires Satan injected not some wrong desire, but Allah shall bring to nought that which Satan has suggested." (Sūratul-Ḥajj, xxii. 51[1].)

We do not wish to discuss a youthful essay on the explanation of these difficulties, put forward by some pious commentators who say that: "Allah commanded several things which were, for good reasons, afterwards revoked and abrogated." Those abrogated passages of the Qurân are distinguished by many of the rigid commentators, into three kinds, "the first, where the letter and the sense are both abrogated; the second, where the letter only is abrogated, but the sense remains; and the third, where the sense is abrogated, though the letter remains." These subtleties of the theological schools do not afford a profitable subject of study for a serious critic.

The most important question in the study of the Qurân is its unchallengeable authenticity. In this theme, the first step would be the following question: How could Muḥammad in all the wars by which his life was so unfortunately agitated, in all the displacements that he must have undergone, keep all the verses which had been previously revealed to him in his memory, after an interval of several years? A plausible and final answer will probably never be given to this question, and the only tenable hypothesis is that which discards the difficulty by the assumption of the prodigious memory of his followers, who are believed to have learnt the strophes by heart, and that in a period lasting from 612 till 632. This hypothesis, which seems to be that of a *dernier ressort*, can be

---

[1] وما ارسلنا من قبلك من رسول ولا نبي الا اذا تمنى القى الشيطان في امنيته فينسخ الله ما يلقي الشيطان

supported by the fact that the Prophet, who was more probably an unlettered man[1], had never thought of writing a book, or of gathering together, in a complete code, the scattered verses which he had recited to his friends, in some circumstances of his life; so much so, that after his death, the emissaries of Abu Bekr, his successor in the Caliphate, could scarcely put together some separate bits of verses, despite the good memory, and the extreme care of Zaid ibn Thâbit, the real compiler of the Qurân of to-day.

This historical fact is suggested by the first refusal of Zaid to undertake the compilation of the Qurân, on the ground that the Prophet himself had never done so. "What right have I," said Zaid to Abu Bekr, "to gather in the form of a book what the Prophet has never intended to transmit to posterity by this channel? And since the Prophet never designed to give his message in this way, is it a lawful work that I am commanded to do?"

As to the prodigious memory of Eastern people who imperturbably and faithfully preserve verses of songs and poems, in their daily life, during a long space of time, we must say that this fact has been a little exaggerated; and nearly always the rural ditties, used in our day among the Bedawin and the Kurdish population of the plains of Syria and Mesopotamia, are recited by different tribes in a different way, and the changes are often more or less sensible according to the remoteness of the tribes one from the other. So, for instance, how many significant various readings can we find in the well-known Arabic elegy called *'Itâbah*, in the divers Bedawin tribes of Albu-Ḥamad, Shammar, 'Aniza, Dleim? etc. and, besides the various readings, how many new couplets of the Kurdish glee called *Mamo Zîné* are used in the deadly sept of Mîra, which are absolutely unknown in the tribes of Hâja, Zêwiki, Shakâki? etc.

As to the faithfulness of a tradition among Eastern people, it has been, I think, accentuated too strongly, and the best comparison for this string of traditions would be, to anyone who has travelled in the arid deserts, a great caravan of big camels walking one after another, but all being guided by a small donkey. We cannot, indeed, understand why Eastern people should deviate in this matter from the natural law of a progressive evolution, and the tenacity with which some people cling to ancient religious creeds and habits of daily life, has nothing to do with the change of words and the exaggeration of historical details; and for that matter, a serious man, who knows the domestic life of the nomads, will doubtless ascertain that the donkey, which conducts the imposing caravan of camels, is sometimes smaller in the East than in the West.

Besides the ordinary channel of the wonderful memory of the Arabs, many

[1] Muḥammad often calls himself "the unlettered prophet" (النبي الامي). Cf. Nöldeke, *ibid.* p. 10.

verses have been transmitted to Zaid by writing, a kind of writing which was in use at Mecca in the time of the Prophet; but since we cannot explain why some verses should have been written and others not, and specially since we are not told which are the verses transmitted to Zaid by writing, and which are those that he knew only from memory, this fact cannot come, till fuller light dawns, into the sphere of a scientific and positive study. To believe that several verses of the Qurân were written by friends of the Prophet during his lifetime, is in accordance with some phrases of this sacred book which mention clearly the name of *Kitâb* "what is written, scriptures," but to state that the fragmentary revelations were almost entirely written and "put promiscuously into a chest[1]" is in contradiction to the kind of life that Muḥammad led, and to early and authentic sources. In accepting such low and hardly disinterested traditions of Moslem authors, why should we not regard as true other and not less authoritative narratives which inform us that all the Sūrahs were completed according to the directions of the angel Gabriel, who, on the other hand, brought only to Muḥammad, in parcels, a text written on a table of "vast bigness," styled the *Preserved Table* and existing from all eternity near Allah's throne? Muḥammadan pious annalists know, too, that a copy made from this eternal original, has been sent to the lowest heaven, whence Gabriel was accustomed to shew it once a year[2] to the Prophet, bound in silk and adorned with gold and precious stones of Paradise. The Prophet himself puts into the mouth of God the following sentences: "By the Luminous Book!—We (Allah) have made it an Arabic Qurân that ye may understand; and it is a transcript of the Archetypal Book kept by us" (Sūratuz-Zukhruf, xliii. 1–3), and again: "We ourselves (Allah) have sent down to thee the Qurân as a missive from on high" (Sūratud-Dahr, lxxvi. 23), and again: "That this is the honourable Qurân, written on the *Preserved Table*; let no one touch it but the purified" (Sūratul-Wâḳi'ah, lvi. 77–78), and again: "Say, the Holy Spirit hath brought it down with truth, from thy Lord." Sūratun-Naḥl (xvi., v. 104), etc., etc.

We know that the whole text of the Qurân has been drawn up twice by Zaid ibn Thâbit, who, it is said, was the amanuensis of the Prophet. The first recension was made under the Caliphate of Abu Bekr, and at the instigation of 'Omar, his successor, between 11 and 15 A.H. "I fear," said this true believer, to the Caliph, "that slaughter may again wax hot amongst the reciters of the Qurân, on other fields of battle, and that much may be lost therefrom. Now therefore my advice is, that thou shouldst give speedy orders for the collection of

---

[1] G. Sale, *The Koran*, Preliminary discourse, p. 46.

[2] He shewed it to him twice in his last year.

the Qurân." Abu Bekr agreed, and addressing Zaid ibn Thâbit, he said, "Thou art a young man, and wise; against whom no one amongst us can cast an imputation. Wherefore now search out the Qurân, and bring it together." Yielding to the joint entreaties of Abu Bekr and 'Omar, Zaid sought out the fragments of the Qurân from every quarter and gathered them together, from date-leaves, bits of parchment, tablets of white stone, and from the hearts of men[1].

The Qurân, so collected and drawn up by Zaid, was committed by 'Omar to the custody of his own daughter Ḥafṣa, the Prophet's widow. We are not told, by any contemporary outside writer, of what kind were these tablets of white stone, or these date-leaves, and the early sources do not suggest that the Prophet had ever used such materials. It is quite possible, therefore, that the only source which Zaid had for the greater part of the text was "the hearts of men," and some scattered scraps of parchment. This hypothesis is supported by the absolute want of any chronological order in the Qurân; and this want suggests to us the idea that the book is not a result of one source of information, or of one Arab reciter, and that it has not been written in deep and laborious study, but that it is simply the outcome of many different recitals that Zaid heard day by day, and gradually wrote down in the measure and proportion that he received them. One day he received some verses "from the breast" of some inhabitants of Medîna dealing with the life of the Prophet in that city, and he wrote them quickly in his book; the next day, hearing some other recitals from some inhabitants of Mecca, he embodied them with the previous verses revealed in Medîna. For this reason, we can scarcely find a long Sūrah of the Qurân which is not twice or thrice at least composite, *i.e.* having verses dating from the time when the Prophet was still in his native town, and some others referring to the time immediately following his flight to Yathrib. It is highly probable, too, that the bits of parchment used by Zaid contained sometimes a complete narrative of a biblical incident, and that the only work of the compiler was to put such well digested material in one of the Sūrahs of the book that he edited. In this category must be counted all the verses dealing with the history of Joseph, of the birth of the Christ, and many other stories.

Finally, if we understand correctly the following verse of Sūratul-Ḥijr (xv. 90–91): "As we sent down upon (punished) the dividers (of the Scripture?) who broke up the Qurân into parts[2]," we are tempted to state that, even when the

---

[1] See *Fihrist*, ed. by G. Flügel, p. 24. Other traditions: افواه الرجال وجريد النخل والجلود

[2] كما انزلنا على المقتسمين. الذين جعلوا القرآن عضين

Prophet was alive, some changes were noticed in the recital of certain verses of his sacred book. There is nothing very surprising in this fact, since Muḥammad could not read nor write, and was at the mercy of friends for the writing of his revelations, or, more frequently, of some mercenary amanuenses.

The book, drawn up by this method, continued to be the authoritative and standard text till about 29–30 A.H. under the Caliphate of 'Othmân. At this time the wonderful faithfulness of Arab memory was defective, and according to a general weakness of human nature, the *Believers* have been heard reciting the verses of the Qurân in a different way. This fact was due specially, it is said, to the hundreds of dialects used in Arabia. Zaid was again asked to put an end to these variations which had begun to scandalize the votaries of the Prophet. That indefatigable compiler, assisted by three men from the tribe of Ḳuraish[1], started to do what he had already done more than 15 years before. The previous copies made from the first one written under Abu Bekr were all destroyed by special order of the Caliph: the Revelation sent down from heaven was one, and the book containing this Revelation must be one.

The critic remarks that the only guarantee of the authenticity of the Qurân is the testimony of Zaid; and for this reason, a scholar who doubts whether a given word has been really used by Muḥammad, or whether it has been only employed by Zaid on his own authority, or on the meagre testimony of some Arab reciters, does not transgress the strict laws of high criticism. If the memory of the followers of the Prophet has been found defective from the year 15 to 30 A.H. when Islâm was proclaimed over all Arabia, why may it not have been defective from 612 to 632 A.D. when the Prophet was often obliged to defend his own life against terrible aggressors? And if the first recension of Zaid contained always the actual words of Muḥammad, why was this compiler not content with re-establishing it in its entirety, and why was the want of a new recension felt by 'Othmân? How can it be that in the short space of 15 years, such wonderful variants could have crept into the few copies preceding the reign of the third Caliph that he found himself bound to destroy all those he could find? If 'Othmân was certainly inspired only by religious purposes, why did his enemies call him "The tearer of the Books"? and why did they fasten on him the following stigma: "He found the Qurâns many and left one; he tore up the Book[2]"? We deem, therefore, as too categorical the following verdict

---

[1] The annalists know them to be 'Abdallah ibn Zobair, Sa'îd ibn Al-'Aṣ, and 'Abdur-Raḥmân ibn Al-Ḥâreth, followers of the Prophet (*Fihrist*, p. 25).

[2] Ṭabari, I. 2952, 10; II, 516, 5; and Yāḳūt, *Dictionary of learned men*, VI. 300, 499; see D. S. Margoliouth's *The early development of Mohammedanism*, 1914, p. 37.

of Von Hammer: "We hold the Qurân to be as surely Muḥammad's word, as the Muḥammadans hold it to be the word of God."

Though a convincing answer worthy of *twentieth* century criticism cannot be given to the preceding questions, we believe that Zaid endeavoured to reproduce, faithfully, so far as he could, the very words of Muḥammad. The imperfections of all kinds, and the want of historical order found in his book, are terrible witnesses against his intellectual proficiency; but, on the other hand, the fragmentary qualities of the last Sūrahs, the good control of the first Caliphs, and especially the suitable time of his compilation, when many believers were able to recite several verses by heart, testify to his faithfulness. We believe too, that if the historical attainments of the first Moslems and of Zaid himself had been less restricted, they would perhaps have modified in some way the historical and topographical errors which the Qurân contains.

Now, at what date has the Qurân been arranged in the order that it follows in our day? Professor D. S. Margoliouth remarks very justly that "the task of arranging the sacred texts in fixed groups might very well have appalled a Moslem; we could scarcely credit a contemporary of the Prophet with having the courage to attempt it. On the other hand, the notion that the Sūrahs existed as frames, which gradually became filled as revelations descended, has little to commend it, and involves the existence of an official copy, which we have seen to be excluded by the evidence[1]." We maintain, however, that this arrangement was made at the time of the first recension, and not at the second; the scandal which would have followed it at the time when the Qurân was known by many a Muḥammadan, and specially by believers in foreign countries, makes the contrary hypothesis very improbable.

"The recension of 'Othmân has been handed down to us unaltered. So carefully, indeed, has it been preserved, that there are no variations of importance —we might almost say no variations at all—to be found in the innumerable copies scattered throughout the vast bounds of the Empire of Islâm; contending and embittered factions, taking their rise in the murder of 'Othmân himself, within a quarter of a century after the death of Mahomet, have ever since rent the Moslem world; yet but *one Coran* has been current amongst them; and the consentaneous use by all of the same scripture, in every age, to the present day, is an irrefragable proof that we have now before us the very text prepared by command of the unfortunate Caliph. There is probably no other work in the world which has remained for 12 centuries with so pure a text....It is one of the maxims of the Moslem world (supported perhaps by Sura xi. 2) that the Coran is incorruptible, and that it is preserved from error and variety

[1] Margoliouth, *Mohammedanism*, pp. 69–70.

of reading by the miraculous interposition of God himself....According to the orthodox doctrine, every syllable of the Coran is of divine origin, eternal and uncreate as the Deity itself[1]."

From what we have said in the preceding pages, it is evident that if we find a manuscript of the Qurân presenting various readings of consonants and of complete words, and more specially if this manuscript offers some interpolations and omissions, it would not be too rash to suppose that it goes back to a pre-'Othmânic period. The conclusion is clear and is corroborated by the constant history of the Muḥammadan world, from the VIIth century down to our own day.

Viewing the linguistic wording of the text of the Qurân, we desire to examine a question which concerns us more than the others. Does the Qurân contain the flower of the Arabic language, and is the challenge given by the Prophet himself true? Besides the sentences quoted in the preceding pages, the Prophet repeats several times with a certain emphasis: "We gave a Qurân written in Arabic; it is in Arabic that this Qurân has been revealed, etc.[2]" Philologists will not be much offended, if we send our reader, for an answer to this question, to the excellent works of a man who deserves the gratitude of every Orientalist, Th. Nöldeke, and chiefly to his *Geschichte des Qorâns* already mentioned. We would wish only to draw attention to the following remarks:

"The Arabic literature preceding the epoch of the Prophet is imperfectly known; but we may be allowed to state that it was not very flourishing, since the traces that it left for future generations are scanty in comparison with the formidable swarm of useful lucubrations of the post-Muḥammadan time. This being so, the Moslem authors are not to be blamed when they call that time the epoch of *Ignorance*[3] though they mean specially, by this qualification, an ignorance about Allah and his immediate attributes. The works of the best writers have been collected at the beginning of the IXth century by Aṣma'i and are Ṭarafa, Amrul-Ḳais, 'Antara, Zuhair, Nâbigha, 'Alḳama[4]." If we add to this number Ta'abbaṭa-Sharran[5] and Shanfarâ and some others found in the book of Louis Cheikho[6] but with some restriction about the authenticity of all their poems we may have the approximate number.

---

1 Muir, *Life of Mahomet*, 1894, pp. xiv, xxi–xxii.

2 Expressions such as قرآنا عربيا or حكما عربيا etc. are sometimes used in the Qurân.

3 In Arabic الجاهلية.

4 Edit. of W. Ahlwardt, *The Divans of the six ancient Arabic poets* (1870).

5 In Arabic تابط شرا.

6 *Les poètes Arabes chrétiens* (1890), cf. another Arabic book of the same writer, *Le Christianisme et la littérature Chrétienne en Arabie avant l'Islâm* (1912). Everybody knows the conscientious studies of Sir Charles Lyall, on this subject.

Now when we compare the style, the method of elocution, the purity of vocables, the happy adjustment of words, the choice of good rhymes in these pre-Islâmic writings with the Qurân, we are often tempted to give them an unchallengeable superiority; and it is only the kind of life, foreign to all learning, that can explain the great uneasiness that the author of the Qurân shews when he wishes to write in rhyme, and finds himself short of common lexicographical terms. So in Sūratul-Jinn the author had certainly an intention to write in rhymed prose (*saj'*), but his linguistic knowledge failing him, he repeats the word احدا six times at the end of 28 short sentences. Besides the repetitions, being quite short of rhymes, even through this method, he changes the letter *Dâl* to a *bâ'* in *vv.* 5, 8, 15, to a *qâf* in *vv.* 6, 13, 16. This example, chosen amongst hundreds of others which are found frequently in the final Sūrahs, is not weakened by some foreign and cacophonic terms of which the author of the Qurân is enamoured, ex. gr. سلسبيلا Sūrah lxxvi. 18; فرقان from the Aramaic ܦܘܪܩܢܐ Sūrah viii. 42; ii. 181; iii. 2 *et passim*; غسلين (!) Sūrah lxix. 36; سجين (!) lxxxiii. 7, 8; قمطريرا lxxvi. 70; الطاغوت Sūratun-Nisâ (iv. 78 *et passim*) inspired from the Aramaic ܛܥܘܬܐ; الحواريين Sūratul-Mâidah (v. 111–112, etc.) from the corresponding Ethiopic root, etc., etc.[1] We believe, moreover, that it is by the want of good literary attainments that we can explain the vulgar disfigurement of the names John (Yoḥannan), Jesus (Esho') into يحيى *Iaḥya* and عيسى *'Îsa*. Muḥammad seems to have taken the vulgar form of these names given in the popular language to children by some Christians of Jewish descent just as in English the name of Margaret becomes in colloquial fashion, Margie (*Scottice*, Maggie, Meg, Peggie), that of Elizabeth, Lizzie or Bessie, and Robert, Bob or Bertie.

Another and not less wonderful instance of spelling is used in Sūratut-Tîn, where the name of Mount Sinai (in Arabic سيناء as in Sūratul-Mū'minîn, xxiii. 20), is written سينين (!) to make it rhyme with the preceding verse and the following one, والتين والزيتون. وطور سينين وهذا البلد الامين The disfigurement, too, of the name of Elijah (in Arabic الياس as in Sūratul-An'âm, vi. 85) into الياسين (!) to make it rhyme with the final words of the phrase, suggests on this point a systematic habit on the part of the Prophet:

سلام على الياسين: انا كذلك نجزي المحسنين.

(Sūratuṣ-Ṣâfât, xxxvii. 130.)

This disfigurement of proper nouns is sometimes used in such an awkward manner that, if we wish to set aside an interminable tergiversation, we must

---

[1] Cf. S. Fraenkel, *De vocalibus in antiquis Arabum carminibus et in Corano peregrinis*, 1880, p. 23 *et passim*.

attribute the origin of some unknown names, so strangely altered, to Muḥammad's own invention. So, who will easily be convinced that the Hūd of Sūratul-A'râf (vii. 63 *et pas.*) is the same man as the Eber of the Bible[1], that the Ṣâleḥ of Sūrat Hūd (xi. 64, etc.) is the same man as Peleg of Genesis (xi. 16)[2], and that the Shu'aib of Sūratush-Shu'arâ (xxvi. 177, etc.) is the same name as Hobab[3] (Numb. x. 29)? No tradition, however corrupted it might have been, would have altered these biblical names in such a wonderfully different mould.

Other alterations of names may perhaps be sufficiently explained by a traditional Christian or Jewish channel; so in Sūratul-An'âm (vi. 74) Terah, Abraham's father, is called "Azar," and we know that in some Judaeo-Christian circles, Terah was called "Athar[4]." The Djâlūt, too, of Sūratul-Baqarah (ii. 250) is unmistakably Goliath; likewise, the Ḳârūn of Sūratul-Qaṣaṣ (xxviii. 76) seems to be the Korah of the Bible. At any rate, philology will be, for a long time, unable to explain convincingly how the name of Saul could become Ṭâlūt, as in Sūratul-Baqarah (ii. 248, 250), nor how the name of Enoch could become Idrîs, as in Sūrat Mariam (xix. 57, etc.), nor, finally, how the name of Obadiah (1 Kings xviii. 4) or of Ezechiel could become Dhul-Kifl, as in Sūratul-Anbiâ' (xxi. 85), in spite of a brilliant suggestion that Ezechiel is called by the Arabs Kefil (!)[5].

In any case, whatever view we may take of the claims of Muḥammad, no one can deny that he was a great man, ranking with men of the highest genius, as a skilful administrator after the Eastern fashion, and wielding every kind of spiritual weapon to attract and captivate his hearers and his countrymen. His legislation, though perhaps too theocratic for the democratic spirit of our day, was perfection at the time when he lived; *Exitus acta probat.* A man who put an end, in less than 10 years, to two formidable kingdoms, the kingdom of the old Achemenides represented by the classic Sassanides, and that of the Roman Caesars of Eastern countries, by means of some camel-drivers of Arabia, must be, at any rate, taken into consideration[6]. A controller of conscience and soul to so many millions, and in the plain light of civilisation, is indeed greater than Alexander and Bonaparte known only to-day in historical books. The proclamations of a semi-nomad Arab of the obscure town of Mecca have been recited by the wide Islâmic world thirteen centuries ago, and are recited to-day;

---

[1] Ita Geiger, *Oper. sup. laud.* pp. 113–119.

[2] This name is perhaps an echo of *Shelah*.

[3] Ita M. Rodwell, *The Koran*, p. 109.

[4] Cf. Maracci, *Prodr.* IV. p. 90.

[5] In Niebuhr's *Travels*, II. p. 265.

[6] The Persian poet Sa'di calls him *the earth conquering horseman with his chestnut Burâq*:

سوار جهانگیر یکران براق

even the cross of the Messiah has been for many years nearly eclipsed by the Crescent, and the name of the *Praised One* of Arabia has been on many occasions on the point of overrunning the last refuge of Christianity. What history is unable to find, even in the XXth century, is a name more terrible than that of *Muḥammad.*

II

For a scientific comprehension of the text of the Qurân, three kinds of study may be found useful: (1) The commentators of the Qurân; (2) the grammarians who applied to it the Arabic vowels and diacritical points; (3) the divers forms of script formerly used in the Arabic language.

When the semi-nomad Arabs started to conquer the world, they did not carry with them, on their camels, any productions of a progressive and latent literature, for they were not brought up in high schools of science and philology. The most picturesque figure amongst these first Arabs is that of the Caliph 'Omar entering the holy city of Jerusalem (637), mounted on his camel, a bag of dates and a skin of water by his side; this provision being judged sufficient for his simple wants. It is worth observing how exactly the Aramaeo-Syrian population of that period of conquests called these Arabs by derision: *Hagarians*, *Ishmaelites*, with the purpose of indicating precisely the semi-barbarous literary education that they had received[1]. But an end was soon made to this awkward situation; and the intelligent Arabs, attracted by the example of their neighbours, began to spread everywhere the language of the Qurân, and to devote themselves to the sciences which had long given to their new fellow-countrymen an unchallenged superiority. A well-known Syriac writer, Bar Hebraeus, tells us a significant fact, that the Umayyad Caliph Walîd ordered that the official acts of Damascus should henceforth be drawn up in Arabic, and no longer in Greek[2]. The sanguinary battles of Yarmûk (636) and Kadesia (637) in imposing a new rule over the remains of the once classic empires, gave them a new sacred language.

With regard to the commentaries on the Qurân, the only question in Arabic literature which concerns our subject, they are very important for the criticism of the text, since the commentators, when quoting and explaining a given verse in their books, quote it faithfully, and they often try to discuss it with all the resources of their science, literally and spiritually. The first commentator of the early epoch of Islâm, was Ibn 'Abbâs, cousin of Muḥammad, who seems

[1] Cf. A. Mingana, *Sources Syriaques*, vol. I. part II. p. 182 sqq.

[2] *Chron. Syr.* edit. Bruns, p. 120; and edit. Bedjan, p. 115.

to have been the main source of the traditional exegesis of the Qurân. On theological grounds, a great number of his opinions have been considered heretical. He and his disciples deal with the sense and connexion of a complete verse, and neglect the literal meaning of a separate word. His commentaries are therefore what Christian writers would call more spiritual than literal. No complete commentary either by the relatives of the Prophet or by extraneous writers has come down to us from this period.

The greatest commentator of a later generation is the well-known Ṭabari (839–923 A.D.[1]). He is a mine for the knowledge of the wide Islâmic legislation, and has sometimes excellent views about the occasion of the revelation of several verses. He is first of all a historian, availing himself of the method of *Isnâd*, and by this channel he preserves several interesting traditions of the early age of Muḥammadanism.

Another good commentator is Az-Zamakhshari[2] (1075–1144). He is, according to the judgment of Nöldeke, too subtle a man, trying to apply his rhetorical and philosophical theories to the most practical of men: Muḥammad.

In our own days, the commentary most used by Moslem theologians is that of Al-Baiḍhâwi (†1286) who employed the same method as that of Az-Zamakhshari in a more methodical manner.

The end of the XIIIth century, which marks the decadence and the close of the 'Abbâsside Caliphate, marks, too, the apogee of the Arabic investigations in the Qurân. The numerous commentators of a later date content themselves with quoting, abridging the old authors, and writing books more popular than original.

A good commentary needs good reading, and good reading, in the Semitic languages, involves an accurate knowledge of the right position of the vowels, with all the orthoepical signs of punctuation. We ought to say at once that according to the measure of scientific investigations of to-day, the Arabs, apart from seven or ten marks of intonation, never used the *rhetorical signs* employed sometimes so fantastically and so awkwardly by the Aramaeans. The Arabic language possessing a kind of inflection like the Greek and the Latin, did not experience any great necessity for reaching even the fortieth part of the frightful number forty that the Aramaeans have invented for an intelligent reading of their Bible, and which are called by the curious and general name of *Puḥâmés*[3] "similarities, comparisons." A practical reason must have deterred the Arabs from adopting such a complicated system, and this reason is found in the script

[1] Recently (1903) edited in Cairo, in 30 parts.
[2] Edited in Calcutta (1859) by Nassau-Lees.
[3] See A. Mingana, *Clef de la langue Araméenne*, 1905, pp. 33–34.

of their language which distinguishes several consonants by means of one, two or three dots placed either under or over a letter. The adoption of the *Puḥâmês* of the Aramaeans would have created an insurmountable mental difficulty in distinguishing a diacritical point from an orthoepical one dealing specially with a proper accent of voice in the reading of a sentence.

While the Aramaeans and the Hebrews admitted several vowels and invented a special sign for every vowel pronounced open or closed, short or long, the prudent Arabs adopted only three vowels, but these three vowels, represented by a stroke of the pen under or over the letter, respond quite sufficiently to all philological exigencies, since each one of them, when followed by a weak letter, is considered as long, ex. gr. زَارُونِي "they have visited me," and it is considered short, when followed by a letter which is not quiescent, ex. gr. قُتِلَ "he has been killed," and it is shortly closed when followed by a quiescent or reduplicated letter, ex. gr. إِخْتَرْتُمْ "you have chosen." By this method, every vowel becomes quantitatively three, and so the system is more ingenious than that of the Hebrews, and of the Aramaeans, who by a long use and borrowing very often neglected the short vowel, so important in poetry and in euphonic sounds.

The history of the vowels is somewhat obscure. It is certain that their invention cannot go back to the period preceding the Umayyad Caliphate of Damascus. The period of conquest and of intestine war caused by the crucial question of the divine Caliphate, which covered the Muḥammadan world with blood, at the time of 'Othmân and onwards, was not very suitable for scientific researches. The Umayyad Empire, though distinguished by some great productions of poetry and historical science, is unknown (except for some mere names such as that of Abul-Aswad Ad-Do'ali, or 'Abdur-Raḥmân ibn Ormiz, a Persian scholar, etc.) as a starting point for grammatical and morphological studies. The first period of conquest lasted from the death of the Prophet, 632 to 661 A.D., when Mu'âwiah entered Kūfa and became the sole representative of Muḥammad; the second period from 661 till January 25, 750 A.D., when the battle of Shaharzūr gave the sceptre to the 'Abbâssides. Therefore, till the accession of Saffâḥ, no centre of grammatical learning has left a trace to posterity. But at this time, the two other branches of the Semitic stock, the Israelites and the Aramaeans, had already passed the time of the careful elaboration of their Massorah, and their vowel-system had acquired a firm foundation, being, in fact, almost at the end of its final evolution.

From the middle of the VIth century, the Monophysite, Aḥud-Emmeh, Metropolitan of Tagrit, had opened a path for the Syriac grammar. Some years before him, the famous Joseph of Ahwâz, had established, in the

University of Nisibis, a solid foundation for orthoepical studies and for the right pronunciation of the vowels. In the middle of the VIIth century, a school founded by Abba Sabrowy, at Beth Shehak, near Nisibis, made the Nestorian system of vowels known even among the Monophysites, their enemies. Before 700 A.D. Jacob of Edessa, by his well-known sentence ܒܫܝܢܐ ܬܚܝܐ ܐܘܪܗܝ ܐܡܢ *Edessa, our mother, thou shalt live in quietness*, which represents all the vowels of the Aramaic language used to-day, marks the end of a systematic evolution of phonetic studies in the Syriac grammar. The school of Edessa, the University of Nisibis, the monasteries of Tel'eda, Ḳennešrin, and Ḳarḳaphta, had then made complete, in the period lasting from 450 to 700 A.D., the phonetic essays which the writers of a later period were content to abridge or to modify in some insignificant details[1].

On the other hand, the strong Israelite colony which had remained behind from the old Babylonian captivity vied in a laudable zeal with the Aramaeans. By means of some prudently distributed bribes, they could always secure a satisfactory political condition under the Sassanide Sapor I and his successors. Their prestige was so widely felt that, in the IVth century, they contrived to be favoured by the harem of the Queen Ephra Hormizd, to whom Christian writers of that time attribute the frightful ordeal that Sapor II, the enemy of the Roman legions, inflicted, in 341, on the Christians of the Persian Empire[2]. According to the Talmud, the Jews of Babylonia are from a purer race even than those of Palestine; we read, in fact, in the *Talm. Bab.* under the treatise *Ḳiddušin*, the following sentence[3]: "Tous les pays sont comme de la pâte relativement à la Palestine, mais ce pays l'est relativement à la Babylonie." By the works of Christian writers in Mesopotamia, we know how great was the influence that they exercised in that country and in the neighbouring districts. Of the 23 homilies of Jacob Aphrahaṭ (IVth century) nine are devoted to the anti-Judaic controversy. Narsai (†502) has also some striking discourses against them.

The Torah was always the subject of a special study among the Jews of the Captivity either under the Arsacido-Parthians or under the Sassanido-Persians, but we know that from the third century and onwards the study has been considerably extended. The great *Sidra* of Sora, founded in this epoch, acquired a world-wide renown, and could not be eclipsed by other celebrated schools

---

[1] Cf. M. Merx, *Historia artis grammaticae apud Syros*, Leipzig, 1889. Duval, *Littérature Syriaque*, 3me édit. p. 285 *et seq.*

[2] Cf. Evod. Assemani, *Acta Martyr. Orient.* vol. I. pp. 19, 54 etc. Nöldeke, *Geschichte der Perser und Araber zur Zeit der Sassaniden aus der Arabischen Chron. des Tabari*, p. 68, n. 1.

[3] Quoted in Neubauer's *Géographie du Talmud*, p. 320.

established at Nehardea, Perozšabur, Maḥôzé (Seleucia) and Pumbaditha[1]. The Rabbinic Massorah flourished in these centres, if not more than in the highest schools of Galilee, at least in an equal degree with them, and the scientific investigations of Babylonian Jews contributed more to the final fixing and delimitation of the complicated Massoretic system as we have it to-day, than the researches of any other writers. In several MSS. of the Old Testament, the work of these Israelite centres of learning is designated by the gloss מדנח *the East*, and we know that in the sacred books of the Jews, the "Babylonian punctuation" is in many cases better even than the "Tiberian punctuation."

When the 'Abbâsside dynasty appeared in the East, and new Caliphs settled in Baghdâd, the grammatical studies of their neighbours were then at their apogee. The intestine dissensions about the Caliphate having been at last cut short by the two-edged sword of Abu Muslim a new and deeper direction of studies was given to Arabic phonetics and morphology. Two celebrated centres of Arabic studies soon flourished in Southern Mesopotamia: the school of Baṣrah and that of Kūfa. We do not wish our readers to understand that we positively deny that these two schools may have existed before the accession of the 'Abbâsside dynasty, but it is quite certain that to assign their foundation to the time immediately following Muḥammad's death, as some scholars state, and to believe that they exercised an influence as strong as that which they had, at a later time, under the eastern Caliphate, would perhaps overstep the limits of safe criticism.

The first grammarian specially known for Arabic metre is Khalîl ibn Aḥmad (718–791 A.D.) of the school of Baṣrah. Besides having the glory of being considered the first Arabic grammarian, he is believed to have been the inventor, in the latter half of the VIIIth century, of the *hamza*, a semi-guttural consonant, in comparison with the weak Aliph. So far as I know, no complete grammatical treatise of his is extant to-day. Some grammatical sketches are attributed to him by authors of a late date, but their authenticity seems to be more than doubtful[2]. The earliest Arabic grammarian whose works have come down to us is Sibawaihi[3] (753–793 A.D.), a disciple of Khalîl.

The grammarians of the school of Kūfa seem to have paid more attention to the spoken dialect of the Bedawin, and for this reason their attempts could not influence, at the beginning, the right reading of the Qurân and could still less reach, in a later generation, a celebrity like that of the school of Baṣrah, in spite of the illustrious Kisâ'i, Ibn As-Sekkît and Farrâ', who, according to a trustworthy

---

[1] Cf. Graetz, *Histoire des Juifs* (translated by Bloch), 1888, vol. III. p. 165 *et passim*.

[2] See Brockelmann's *Geschich. der Arabischen Litteratur*, I. p. 100, Weimar, 1898.

[3] Edited by H. Derenbourg, Paris, 1881–1889.

tradition, pronounced to his friends the memorable sentence: "I shall die, and there is in my heart something yet unsettled about the particle حتّى." To some extent, their task was very difficult, and to Arabize all the Semitic and Aryan dialects, spoken in the old Chaldaean lands, such as the Mandaitic[1] and the Ḳatrian, was a harder task than many suppose[2].

The foundation of the Arabic vowels is based on the vowels of the Aramaeans. The names given to these vowels is an irrefragable proof of the veracity of this assertion. So the *Phatḥ* (فتح) corresponds in appellation and in sound to the Aramaic *Phtâḥa* (ܦܬܚܐ); the *Khaphedh* (خفض) is exactly the Aramaic *Ḥbâṣa* (ܚܒܨܐ). But though the Arabs imitated the Syrians in the verbal designation of their vowels, they recoiled, and very justly, from the absurd servility to Hellenism of their masters, who, after the time of Christological controversies and onwards, could not shrink from the Greek method; and placing their Morphology and Syntax on fresh bases, they laid the first foundation of a high philology which excites our admiration in the present day. Viewing the intimate formation of words, they divided them into biliteral, triliteral and quadriliteral with essential letters, in such a steady method, that even the strongest philologists of the XXth century are obliged to walk in their steps and to accept their impeccable terminology. Our thanks are due to the sagacity of scholars who in a short period of time perfected the delicate science of the deep constitution of their language.

The sagacity of the professors in the two schools of Baṣrah and of Kūfa was for a number of years challenged by a high seat of learning which the 'Abbâssides established in Baghdâd and which flourished greatly from the beginning of the IXth century and onwards under the control of Christian physicians. This new school acquired a decided superiority over the others, because it taught several sciences derived from Greek and Syriac books translated into Arabic by the group of Nestorian doctors of the family of Bokhtîsho', Ḥunain and Maswai[3]. Physicians have always had a preponderating authority at the courts of Eastern monarchs, and going back into past history, we shall find one man, Gabriel the Drustbed, eclipsing the prestige of all the formidable Dyophysite community, in the palace of the Sassanide Chosroes II Parwez[4].

---

[1] About the relations of the Mandaeans with Christianity, see Brandt, *Die Mandäische Religion, ihre Entwickelung und Geschichtliche Bedeutung*, pp. 140–145 *et passim*.

[2] For a general view on Arabic Literature, the reader will find good information in R. A. Nicholson's *A literary history of the Arabs*, 1907; for some particular details, several articles written, in Arabic, in the review *Al Machriq*, Beirut, seem to be well documented and scientific.

[3] See *Ibn Abi Uṣaibi'ah*, vol. I. p. 175 *et passim*. Bar Hebraeus, *Chron. Syr.* pp. 134 and 162.

[4] See Labourt, *Le Christianisme dans l'empire Perse* (1904), p. 219 sqq.

The first discoverer of the Arabic vowels is unknown to history. The opinions of Arab authors, on this point, are too worthless to be quoted; the critics of our day, too, have not clearly established their position on this subject. To find a way of unravelling this tangled question, and to discern the truth among so many positively expressed opinions, is by no means an easy task. If we may advance an opinion of our own, we think that a complete and systematic treatise on these vowels was not elaborated till the latter half of the VIIIth century, and we believe that such an attempt could have been successfully made only under the influence of the school of Baghdâd, at its very beginning. On the one hand, besides the insufficiency of the grounds for assuming an earlier date, we have not a manuscript which can be shewn to be before that time, adorned with vowels; on the other hand, the dependence of these vowels on those of the Aramaeans obliges us to find a centre where the culture of the Aramaic language was flourishing, and this centre is the school of Baghdâd, which was, as we have already stated, under the direction of Nestorian scholars, and where a treatise on Syriac grammar was written by the celebrated Ḥunain.

As to the forms of the Arabic script (we do not speak of the script used in the pre-Qurânic inscriptions), we can reduce them to three principal divisions: the Kūfi, the Naskhi, and the Kūfo-Naskhi. The Kūfi type is characterized by more square and more compact and united letters, and generally by thicker and bigger strokes of the pen. The Naskhi has smaller, thinner and less compact strokes, and resembles more than other types the writing used, in our days, in printed books. The Kūfo-Naskhi is intermediate between these two scripts[1]. It is often very difficult to know, with certitude, the age of a manuscript only by its being written in one of these three types, since we find many documents written in each one of them and belonging to the same period. For instance in *The Palaeographical Society*[2], we meet with manuscripts written in these three scripts and dating from the VIIIth century; cf. Plates XIX, LIX, V. Therefore, it is very often by the specific characters used in each of these three types, and especially by a more or less use of diacritical points, that we are guided when we ascribe a manuscript to a given epoch[3].

For the diacritical points which distinguish the sound of many Arabic letters one from another, it is very puzzling to find a general and infallible criterion. Since many consonants, like the ض and the ص which are distinguished to-day

[1] See B. Moritz's *Arabic palaeography* (with 188 plates), Cairo, 1906; and L. Cheikho, *Spécimens d'écriture Arabe pour la lecture des manuscrits anciens et modernes*, Beyrout, 1911.

[2] *Facsimiles of ancient manuscripts etc.* Oriental Series, Part II. edited by W. Wright, London, 1877.

[3] Cf. the valuable study of Prof. Brockelmann, in the *Encyclopaedia of Islâm*, vol. I. p. 383 sqq.

Characteristics of the writing in Qurân B.

It has Kūfo-Naskhi letters as in Qurân A, with more diacritical points over the ت and the ن and very seldom any over the غ and the ذ, all the other letters being without them. Their characteristic note is that they are smaller, thinner, and more sloping to the left. The Sūrahs exhibiting, in our manuscript, this kind of script are: Sūrat Hūd (xi.), Sūratur-Ra'd (xiii.), Sūrat Ibrâhîm (xiv.), Sūratul-Ḥijr (xv.), Sūratun-Naḥl (xvi.), Sūratul-Asra (xvii.).

Characteristics of the writing in Qurân C.

Its letters resemble those of Qurân B but they are a little smaller, thinner and taller. The peculiarities which seem to distinguish this type of script are: (1) the final ي which, except in the case of في and some other words, is written in a perpendicular and zigzag form; (2) the final م which is very often united to the words which immediately follow; this junction is used in some other words of this series, and in foll. 151a and 150b of the series of Qurân A (ll. 1, 2 and 4); (3) the complete absence of diacritical points. The Sūrahs written in this kind of script are some parts of Sūratul-A'râf (vii.) and some parts of Sūratut-Taubah (ix.).

Besides these three general types of writing, of which we give a facsimile in this book, we believe that there are some portions of the series Qurân B coming from a different manuscript. The considerations which suggest this idea are: (1) the kind of writing, which is not so thick as that used in other pages of this series; (2) the number of lines, which is not always identical; (3) the points which mark the separation of verses, which have a different form; (4) some words which are not spelt in the same manner. We believe also that even in the series of Qurân A some Sūrahs do not belong to the same manuscript as other Sūrahs do; the reasons why we think so are in most cases the same as those mentioned in the series of Qurân B. Thus it is very probable that the foll. 150 a, 150 b and 151 a which contain some awkwardly united words, come from an outside source.

In addition to these special characteristics that we have enumerated, there are in our scraps of the Qurân some peculiarities common to them all which we wish our readers to observe:

(1) The Arabic hamza, possibly invented, as we have already stated, by Khalîl ibn Aḥmad, is not represented in them, even by the sign which doubles

Characteristics of the writing in Qurân B.

It has Kūfo-Naskhi letters as in Qurân A, with more diacritical points over the ت and the ن and very seldom any over the غ and the ذ, all the other letters being without them. Their characteristic note is that they are smaller, thinner, and more sloping to the left. The Sūrahs exhibiting, in our manuscript, this kind of script are: Sūrat Hūd (xi.), Sūratur-Ra'd (xiii.), Sūrat Ibrâhîm (xiv.), Sūratul-Ḥijr (xv.), Sūratun-Naḥl (xvi.), Sūratul-Asra (xvii.).

Characteristics of the writing in Qurân C.

Its letters resemble those of Qurân B but they are a little smaller, thinner and taller. The peculiarities which seem to distinguish this type of script are: (1) the final ي which, except in the case of في and some other words, is written in a perpendicular and zigzag form; (2) the final م which is very often united to the words which immediately follow; this junction is used in some other words of this series, and in foll. 151a and 150b of the series of Qurân A (ll. 1, 2 and 4); (3) the complete absence of diacritical points. The Sūrahs written in this kind of script are some parts of Sūratul-A'râf (vii.) and some parts of Sūratut-Taubah (ix.).

Besides these three general types of writing, of which we give a facsimile in this book, we believe that there are some portions of the series Qurân B coming from a different manuscript. The considerations which suggest this idea are: (1) the kind of writing, which is not so thick as that used in other pages of this series; (2) the number of lines, which is not always identical; (3) the points which mark the separation of verses, which have a different form; (4) some words which are not spelt in the same manner. We believe also that even in the series of Qurân A some Sūrahs do not belong to the same manuscript as other Sūrahs do; the reasons why we think so are in most cases the same as those mentioned in the series of Qurân B. Thus it is very probable that the foll. 150a, 150b and 151a which contain some awkwardly united words, come from an outside source.

In addition to these special characteristics that we have enumerated, there are in our scraps of the Qurân some peculiarities common to them all which we wish our readers to observe:

(1) The Arabic hamza, possibly invented, as we have already stated, by Khalîl ibn Aḥmad, is not represented in them, even by the sign which doubles

the vowel points generally used in the oldest MSS. of the Qurân. Sometimes and in some places where the word may cause an equivocal meaning, instead of a hamza, we have simply a ي, ex. gr. لين for لئن since without this ي this particle would easily be confounded with that of the negative of the future tense لن; again in fol. 161 b we have ايمة because without this *yâ*, which takes the place of a hamza, we would read the word as امة "nation." When there is no fear of ambiguity, there is not even a trace of this strong consonant, ex. gr. (fol. 159 a) يومذ for يومئذ; (fol. 55 b) ولتسلن for ولتسألن; (*ibid.*) تستنسوا for تستأنسوا; (fol. 160 a) يسوا for يئسوا etc.

(2) The ordinary marks of intonation, and the old Massoretic signs are also quite absent. In the oldest MSS. of the sacred book, the *Shadda* is expressed by a sign resembling a coarse Arab number, eight or seven; the *Waṣla* is expressed by a stroke of the pen upon the last letter of the first word, and the *Madda* is very often expressed by a horizontal line; but all these signs, so far as I know, are not found in our text.

(3) We were unable to find in these manuscripts even a shadow of a vowel. We know, too, that in the oldest manuscripts of the Qurân, the signs of vowels are very often represented by some dots, usually red, placed above or under the letter, and in the case of a *Ḍhamma*, between the first letter and that which immediately follows it; these marks are not found in the series A and C, and are very seldom seen in the series B.

(4) So far as I could ascertain, the red circles with the red dots which mark a greater division in the sacred text, are absolutely unknown to our scribes, as we stated above.

(5) Our manuscripts divide always the words, at the end of a line, in such an awkward fashion, that we are tempted to believe that the ancient Syrian and Hebrew copyists had a certain superiority over the first Arab scribes in the art of arranging their sacred books; ex. gr. foll. 98 and 99, the words يسرف and ربك are divided into يسر and ف and ر and بك, etc., etc. without any indication that they belong to each other.

(6) The long vowels (حروف المد) expressed by means of a و and a ي, as in the Aramaic language, are generally represented in our manuscripts, ex. gr. غفور, رحيم, حليم, etc. The case is different with the long vowel *â* which is generally represented in the Aramaic Massorah by means of two perpendicular dots without an Alaph, ex. gr. عبد for عباد, اولد for اولاد, سيت for سيئات, كلمت for كلمات, etc. This fact establishes, once more, the dependence of the Arab vowels on those of the Aramaeans. The first grammarians noticing that the *Ḥibâṣa* (ܒ݂) and the *Ribâṣa* (ܒ݁) were expressed by means of letters, they expressed them, too,

in their language by the same letters, but for the case of *Zeḳâpha*, since it was not represented generally by letters, they did not represent it at all; and they did not find a usual and obligatory sign for it, at the very beginning, and it was in a later period that the Aliph was invented to represent a long vowel, as the case was also not very rare in some old Syriac manuscripts.

This remark may be applied even to the rules dealing with the weak letters, called by the Arab grammarians قواعد الاعلال. These rules systematized in the schools of Baṣrah, Kūfa, and Baghdâd, are not maintained by our manuscripts, since we have, for instance, هديه for هداه (fol. 101, l. 9), and افاصفيكم for افاصفاكم (fol. 99b, l. 8). But what distinguishes the orthography of some of our scraps of the Qurân from some other old Arabic MSS. is the case of this long Aliph in the vocative particle يا "O" which is joined to the following word by means of the complete rejection of the second letter, ex. gr. ينوح instead of يانوح "O Noah" (fol. 107a); يقوم instead of ياقوم "O people" (fol. 106b, ll. 2, 5); يموسى instead of يا موسى "O Moses" (fol. 59a, l. 3).

The diacritical points, as we have already said, in the series of Qurân C are utterly wanting. For the series of Qurân B, since we suppose it to be a little more modern than the series A, we think it unnecessary to enumerate all the letters which have one or two dots denoting their identity. We subjoin a list of all the words in series A which have a diacritical sign:

Fol. 149a, l. 1, a dot over the *nūn* of منا
Fol. 149a, l. 4, two dots over the *tâ* of نحست
Fol. 150b, l. 4, a dot over the *nūn* of تنزيل
Fol. 150b, l. 8, two dots over the *tâ* of موتها
Fol. 159a, l. 3, two dots over the *thâ* of للخبيثين
Fol. 159a, l. 6, two dots over the first and the second *tâ* of تستنسوا
Fol. 159a, l. 8, a dot over the *dhâl* of يوذن
Fol. 156a, l. 8, two dots over the *tâ* of يتبعون
Fol. 158b, l. 8, two dots over the *tâ* of ياتل
Fol. 149b, l. 7, a dot over the *nūn* of اذنا
Fol. 152b, l. 4, two dots over the *tâ* of اتيا and قلتا
Fol. 152b, l. 7, two dots over the *tâ* of تقدير
Fol. 152b, l. 10, a dot over the *nūn* of ربنا
Fol. 160a, l. 4, a dot over the *nūn* of ينشي
Fol. 157b, l. 5, two dots over the *tâ* of واتينه

Perhaps a list of 15 diacritical points in 15 foll., written in a Kūfo-Nashki script, may appear too long; I think that MSS. of this type of writing offering fewer diacritical points are very rare in our days.

We know that in the oldest MSS. of the Qurân the number of verses is not always identical; our MSS. can hardly be an exception to this general rule. As to the points of separation placed at the end of one verse, and at the beginning of another, here are some specimens used in the divers series of our portions of the Qurân, with indication of the page and of the line where they can be easily found.

Sūrah vii., fol. 59b, l. 1	////
Sūrah ix., fol. 104a, l. 8	/////
Sūrah xliv., fol. 150b, l. 1	\\\\
Sūrah xli., fol. 152b, l. 4	//////
Sūrah xvii., fol. 102a, l. 7	////

As to the ornaments placed at the end of a Sūrah, our manuscripts are very parsimonious. Sūrah xvii. which begins at the top of fol. 101 b, Sūrah xiv. which similarly begins in fol. 19b, and Sūrah xvi. which begins in the middle of fol. 15b have absolutely no marks to distinguish them, except the space of one line. Sūrah xlv. which begins in the middle of fol. 150b has the following row of six circles: o o o o o o, and Sūrah xli. which begins in fol. 149b has some strokes like these: ~~~~~~~~~~

The reader will easily find that we have followed, as faithfully as we could, the orthography used in our manuscripts. Besides the more scientific character of this method, it enables us to know the kind of spelling used in the early days of Arabic literature. Our transcription will shew شاي for شيء, قرن for قرآن, يناللوا for ينالوا, اذنا for آذاننا, يوحا for يوحى, ان ما for امّا, عيلم (!) for علم, etc. The lines of our transcription correspond exactly to those of the manuscript.

What seems to enhance the value of these scraps of vellum is that when we compare the text that they exhibit with the established *textus receptus* of the Qurân, as known to-day, we find some interesting various readings, and some omissions which, as stated above, will astonish more than one scholar. These various readings and omissions are more or less numerous according to the age of these scraps, that is, they are more accentuated in the series of Qurân A and C for the simple reason that these two series seem to be the more ancient. We will class the various readings roughly into two groups, those which offer a complete word different from that used in the *textus receptus* of the Qurân, and those which by means of one or two consonants, give another meaning to the sentence used in this sacred book and constitute what we mean by the word *variant.*

FIRST GROUP OF VARIANTS.

1	Qurân: Sūratul-Jâthiah, xlv. 18:	شيًا something
	Our MS. Fol. 150 a, l. 6:	هكما in (their) derision
2	Qurân: Sūratut-Taubah, ix. 43:	وتعلم and you will know
	Our MS. Fol. 53 b, l. 9:	ومنهم and who are
3	Qurân: Sūratul-A'râf, vii. 153:	ورحمة and mercy
	Our MS. Fol. 59 b, l. 6:	وسلم and peace (or greeting)
4	Qurân: Sūratul-Jâthiah, xlv. 18:	الله God
	Our MS. Fol. 150 a, l. 6:	اللكم or اللك blow

Unless اللكم (or اللك) means *blow*, *fist*, *boxing*, it is an obscure word. The sentence of the Qurân is as follows: انهم لن يغنوا عنك من الله شيًا "They will not take the place of Allah in anything, for thee (Muḥammad)." Our text is: انهم لن يغنوا عنك من اللكم (اللك or) هكما "In derision, they will not take the place of a blow, for thee." If this sense is rejected, the real meaning of this substantive would be problematic. The *Ḳâmūs* has simply: الضرب باليد مجموعة واللكز والدفع

The abstract substantive هكْم, in its triliteral form instead of the form تفعّل is not much used in the post-Qurânic compositions, but the adjective هكِم is found in good writers.

SECOND GROUP OF VARIANTS.

1	Qurân: Sūratur-Ra'd, xiii. 26:	الله God
	Our MS. Fol. 16 b, l. 9:	والله and God
2	Qurân: Sūratun-Naḥl, xvi. 17:	افلا do not you?
	Our MS. Fol. 15 a, l. 11:	اولا (same meaning)
3	Qurân: Sūratun-Naḥl, xvi. 22:	ايان when?[1]
	Our MS. Fol. 20 a, l. 4:	اين where?
4	Qurân: Sūrat Ibrâhîm, xiv. 3:	ضلال error
	Our MS. Fol. 19 b, l. 7:	ضل (same meaning)
5	Qurân: Sūratul-Ḥijr, xv. 94:	واعرض and oppose thou
	Our MS. Fol. 18 a, l. 10:	واعرضن and do oppose thou (energ.)

[1] Philologically a contraction of اي آن *at what time?*

6	Qurân: Sūratur-Ra'd, xiii. 33:	زين	was adorned
	Our MS. Fol. 16 a, l. 9:	فزين	verily, was adorned (energ.)
7	Qurân: Sūrat Hūd, xi. 24:	الاخسرون	the most in loss (superl.)
	Our MS. Fol. 107 b, l. 3:	لخسرون	verily, in loss (*Lâm* of energ.)
8	Qurân: Sūrat Hūd, xi. 25:	اخبتوا	they humbled (der. form)
	Our MS. Fol. 107 b, l. 4:	خبتوا	(same meaning, prim. form)
9	Qurân: Sūratun-Naḥl, xvi. 38:	فانظروا	and do look
	Our MS. Fol. 13, l. 5:	وانظروا	and look (better in the context)
10	Qurân: Sūratut-Taubah, ix. 36:	فيهن	in them (fem. plur.)
	Our MS. Fol. 60 a, l. 4:	فيها	in them (fem. sing.)
11	Qurân: Sūratun-Naḥl, xvi. 36:	فاصابهم	and it happened to them (masc. sing.)
	Our MS. Fol. 20 b, l. 9:	فاصابتهم	and it happened to them (fem. sing.)
12	Qurân: Sūratut-Taubah, ix. 37:	لايهدي القوم	(God) will not guide the people...
	Our MS. Fol. 60 a, l. 8:	لايهدا لقوم	(God) will not be quiet towards the people...
13	Qurân: Sūratul-Asra, xvii. 52:	ااِنّا	are we?
	Our MS. Fol. 99 a, l. 7:	انّا	we are
14	Qurân: Sūratul-Asra, xvii. 24:	الاتعبدوا	that you might not serve
	Our MS. Fol. 97 b, l. 7:	فلاتعبدوا	do not serve then
15	Qurân: Sūrat Hūd, xi. 31:	اراكم	I find you (perhaps from راى)
	Our MS. Fol. 106 b, l. 7:	اريكم	I shall shew you (perhaps from ارى)
16	Qurân: Sūrat Hūd, xi. 34:	جادلتنا	thou hast disputed with us
	Our MS. Fol. 107 a, l. 3:	جادلت	thou hast disputed
17	Qurân: Sūratul-Asra, xvii. 1:	باركنا حوله	we blessed round it
	Our MS. Fol. 101 b, l. 3:	بركنا حوله	we knelt down round it (cf. ܒܪܟ)[1]

[1] This verb has been inserted here through our desire to know if there was, in early times, a sure philological criterion to distinguish the words from one another, which are distinguished to-day only by a long vowel; our text of the Qurân has many of these words.

18 Qurân: Sūratut-Taubah, ix. 23: ومن and he who
Our MS. Fol. 104 a, l. 9: فمن (same meaning)

19 Qurân: Sūratut-Taubah, ix. 24: لايهدي القوم (God) will not guide the people...
Our MS. Fol. 109 b, ll. 3–4: لايهدا لقوم (God) will not be quiet towards the people...

20 Qurân: Sūratul-Mu'men, xl. 85: فلم يك ينفعهم ايمانهم their faith did not profit to them
Our MS. Fol. 152 a, l. 11: فلم يكن نفعهم ايمانهم (same meaning in the case of the verb نَفَعَ, but with the infinitive نَفْع): their faith was of no utility to them

21 Qurân: Sūratus-Sajdah, xli. 10: فقال لها he said to her
Our MS. Fol. 152 b, l. 3: فقيل لها it has been said to her

22 Qurân: Sūratus-Sajdah, xli. 5: اننا we
Our MS. Fol. 149 b, l. 8: انما verily

23 Qurân: Sūratul-'Ankabūt, xxix. 24: وقال and he said
Our MS. Fol. 160, l. 12: قال he said

24 Qurân: Sūratun-Naḥl, xvi. 95: لجعلكم he would have made you
Our MS. Fol. 55 b, l. 4: جعلكم (same meaning, but without energy)

25 Qurân: Sūratud-Dukkhân, xliv. 44: اثيم iniquitous
Our MS. Fol. 151 a, l. 5: اثم iniquity

26 Qurân: Sūratun-Naḥl, xvi. 24: يسرون they desire
Our MS. Fol. 20 a, l. 7: تسرون you desire (the dots of the *Tâ* are clear)

27 Qurân: Sūratut-Taubah, ix. 54: وما and not
Our MS. Fol. 53 a, l. 2: ما not

28 Qurân: Sūratun-Naḥl, xvi. 112: عملت (the soul) did
Our MS. Fol. 56 a, l. 9: عملته (the soul) did it

29 Qurân: Sūratun-Naḥl, xvi. 30: بلى verily, yes
Our MS. Fol. 13 b, l. 7: بل but

30 Qurân: Sūratun-Naḥl, xvi. 87–8: واذا and if, (and less frequently) when
Our MS. Fol. 55 a, ll. 4, 6: واذ and when, (and less frequently) if

* * *

There is, too, an omission in the standard text of the Qurân. In Sūratun-Naḥl, xvi. 95, we read ولكن يضل مَن يشآء "but He misleads him whom He wishes (to mislead)," our MS. fol. 55 b has the word الله "Allah" between يضل and مَن, so that the sentence runs thus: ولكن يضل الله مَن يشآء "But Allah misleads him whom He wishes (to mislead)."

Let us now examine the interpolations which may be observed in the standard text of the Qurân, and compare them with our MS.

A.

In Sūratut-Taubah, ix. 38, we read يا ايها الذين آمنوا ما لكم اذا قيل لكم انفروا في سبيل الله اثاقلتم الى الارض "O those who believed, what have you (had) when it was said[1] unto you 'Go forth for the religion of Allah[2],' you inclined[3] heavily towards the earth." Our text (fol. 60 a) has يا ايها الذين آمنوا اذا قيل لكم انفروا في سبيل الله اثاقلتم الى الارض "O those who believed, when it has been said[1] unto you 'Go forth for the religion of Allah[2],' you inclined[3] heavily towards the earth." Here the words ما لكم are omitted; they do not suit the context.

B.

In Sūratut-Taubah, ix. 33, there is هو الذي ارسل رسوله "it is He who sent His Apostle." Our MS. (fol. 109 a) had not the word هو "He" originally, but this pronoun has been added in the margin by a different hand.

C.

In Sūratut-Taubah, ix. 36, we read وقاتلوا المشركين كافة كما يقاتلونكم كافة *make war upon all the unbelievers, as they make war upon all of you.* Our text (fol. 60 a, ll. 4–5) has وقاتلوا المشركين كما يقاتلونكم كافة *make war upon unbelievers as they make war upon all of you*, in neglecting the first كافة.

---

1 Or, if it is said.
2 Literally, in the way of Allah.
3 Or, you incline.

It would be worth while to remark here that our manuscripts maintain the Aliph called الالف الفاصلة even when the verb is used in singular, ex. gr. fol. 161 b, l. 9, تتلوا *that thou mightest recite* for تتلو; again on fol. 17 b, l. 6, لتتلوا for لتتلو. On the other hand, we meet in fol. 109 a, l. 5, with لياكلو *verily they eat* instead of لياكلوا without a paragogic Aliph. This orthography, if a singular sense is intended in the former verbs, is highly ambiguous.

We leave the professional palaeographers to assign a definite and final date to these various scraps of parchment. The opinion that some portions of them may date from the very beginning of the VIIIth century is probable, and even alluring and tenable; critics generally own that hesitation and doubt make sometimes an integral part of palaeographical science, which often settles the date of a document only approximately, in centuries and not in precise years. Even if the *terminus ad quem* is fixed in some manuscripts by the date given in their colophon, yet the *terminus a quo* is still problematic, and it is always difficult to state with safety that a style used in the middle of the VIIIth or IXth century might not have been used likewise at the end of the VIIth. *Servatis servandis*, some pages of our palimpsest may appropriate, at any rate, the aureole of a high antiquity and satisfy all the reasonable exigencies of historical researches. In a general sphere of scientific investigation, a man acquainted with historical and philological lucubrations on the sacred book of Islâm, knows with certitude that a manuscript offering "in derision" instead of "something" deserves respect. Would it be possible to make some portions of our manuscript go back to a time preceding the epoch in which the Qurân has been officially edited in a fixed *textus receptus*? Or, if not, are they perhaps a transcription from some scraps of copies which had escaped the persecuting zeal of 'Othmân? A categorical answer, affirmative or negative, would be, on our part, only premature.

In such a delicate matter, a serious caution was imperative; every variant found in the preceding pages has been verified with a magnifying glass, and sometimes by means of a fresh touch with the re-agent, by the learned ladies Mrs Lewis and Mrs Gibson. The reading of an Arabic palimpsest—and the Arabic palimpsests are not very numerous—is far more difficult than that of a Greek or a Syriac one, since whereas in the old Greek letters and in the Estrangelo characters, almost every letter is written separately, or if not, it is formed in a mould different from its neighbours, the Arabic language has many letters united with the preceding or with the following ones, and scarcely distinguishable by a different stroke of the pen. If then, in a contingent future, a scholar, guided by this first decipherment, notices that I have failed once or twice, I beg him to remember me in the following strophe:

لطافت بود کار صاحب دلان : لطافت بود پیشهٔ مقبلان

ALPHONSE MINGANA.

WOODBROOKE, BIRMINGHAM.
May, 1914.

Errata

p. 40, l. 22, put the word الذين at the end of the preceding line.
p. 56, l. 17, take away the dots from the *Tâ* of سیه.

INDEX OF PROPER NAMES

Aaron, xiv, 2, 3
'Abbâs, Ibn, xxv
'Abbâsside, xxvi, xxix
'Abbâssides, xxvii, xxx
Abraham, xxiv, 18, 19, 48, 49
Abram, xiii
Acacius, xiii
Achemenides, xxiv
'Ad, 18, 19, 70, 71
Ahasuerus, xiv
Ahlwardt, W., xxii
Ahwâz, Joseph of, xxvii
Al-'Aṣ, Sa'îd ibn, xx
Alexander, xxiv
'Alkama, xxii
Amrul-Ḳais, xxii
'Aniza, xvii
'Antara, xxii
Aphrahaṭ, Jacob, xxviii
Apocrypha Syriaca, vi
Aqsi, Mosque of, 50, 51
Arab, xix, xx, xxii, xxiv, xxxi, xxxiv, xxxv
'Arabayé, Beith, xiii
Arabia, xiii, xiv, xx, xxiv, xxv
Arabian, 28, 29, 44, 45, 68, 69
Arabic, v, vi, vii, xi, xvii, xviii, xxii, xxiii, xxv, xxvi, xxviii, xxix, xxx, xxxi, xxxii, xxxiii, xxxv, xxxvi, xlii
Arabist, vi
Arabists, vi
Arabize, xxx
Arabs, xiii, xvii, xxiv, xxv, xxvi, xxvii, xxviii, xxx
Aramaean, xxvi, xxxi, xxxiv
Aramaeans, xxvi, xxvii, xxviii, xxx, xxxi, xxxiv
Aramaeo-Syrian, xxv
Aramaic, xxiii, xxviii, xxx, xxxi, xxxiv
Archetypal Book, xviii
Arsacido-Parthians, xxviii
Aryan, xxx
'Aṣ, Sa'îd ibn Al-, xx
Aṣma'i, xxii
Assemani, Evodius, xxviii
Assyria, xiii
Assyrian, vii, xiii
Assyriology, xiv
Aswad, Abul, xxvii
Athar, xxiv
Azâr, xxiv

Babylonia, xxviii
Babylonian, xxviii, xxix
Babylonian Captivity, xxviii
Babylonian Talmud, xxviii
Baghdâd, xxix, xxx, xxxi, xxxv
Baiḍhâwi, Al, xxvi
Bar-Ṣauma, xiii
Baṣrah, xxix, xxx, xxxv
Bedawin, xvii, xxix
Bedjan, xxv
Beḥîra, Rabban, xiv
Bekr, Abu, vii, xvii, xviii, xix, xx
Ben-Sira, x
Bezae, Cod., x
Bloch, xxix
Boktisho', xxx
Bonaparte, xxiv
Brandt, xxx
British Museum, v, ix, x
Brockelmann, Prof., xxix, xxxi
Buraq, xxiv

Caesars, xxiv
Cambridge University, viii, x
Catherine's, St, Convent, v
Chabot, Dr J. B., xiii
Chaldaean, vii, xxx
Cheikho, Louis, xxii, xxxi
China, viii
Chosroes II, xxx
Christ, xix
Christian, v, viii, ix, x, xi, xii, xiii, xiv, xxii, xxiv, xxvi, xxviii, xxx
Christian Arabic, viii
Christianity, xxii, xxv, xxx
Christians, ix, xii, xiii, xiv, xv, xxiii, xxviii, 10, 11
Christological, xxx
Chrysostom, v
Cowley, Dr, v

Damascus, xxv, xxvii
David, 61
Derenbourg, H., xxix
Dhul-Kifl, xxiv
Djalūt, xxiv
Dleim, xvii
Do'ali, Abul-Aswad Ad-, xxvii
Drustbed, Gabriel the, xxx
Duchesne, xiii
Duval, xxviii
Dyophysite, xxx

Eber, xxiv
Eden, 18, 19, 24, 25, 38, 39
Edessa, xxviii
Egypt, xiv
Elijah, xxiii
Elizabeth, Lizzie, Bessie, xxiii
Ellis, W., v
Emmeh, Aḥud-, xxvii
English, xxiii
Enoch, xxiv
Esdras, xiv
Esho', xxiii
Estrangelo Syriac, v, xlii
Europe, x
Exodus, v
Eyre and Spottiswoode, ix
Ezechiel, xxiv
Ezra, xiv, 10, 11

Farrâ', xxix
Fihrist, xix, xx
Flügel, Gustav, x, xix
Fraenkel, S., xxiii

Gabriel, xviii
Galilee, xxix
Gehenna, 10, 11, 14, 15, 16, 17, 18, 19, 24, 25, 36, 37, 50, 51, 52, 53, 56, 57, 72, 73
Geiger, xiii, xxiv
Genesis, v, xxiv
Gibson, Dr Margaret D., vii, x, xlii
Gideon, xiv
Goliath, xxiv
Gospel, xv, xl, 4, 5
Gottheil, M. R., xiv

Graetz, xxix, xxx
Greek, x, xxv, xxvi, xxx, xlii
Greek Septuagint, v

Ḥafṣa, xix
Hagar, xiii
Hagarians, xxv
Hâja, xvii
Ḥamad, Albu-, xvii
Haman, xiv
Hammer, Von, xxi
Harâm, Mosque of the, 8, 9, 10, 11, 50, 51
Ḥâreth, 'Abdur-Raḥmân, ibn Al-, xx
Harris, Dr Rendel, viii
Hebraeus, Bar, xxv, xxx
Hebrew, x, xxxiv
Hebrews, xxvii
Hellenism, xxx
Hira, xi, xiii,
Hishâm, Ibn, xi, xv
Hobab, xxiv
Horae Semiticae, v
Hormizd, Queen Ephra, xxviii
Huart, Cl., xiii
Hūd, xxiv
Hunain, xxx, xxxi, 8, 9
Hûnan, Day of, 8, 9

Iaḥya, xxiii
Ibrâhim, Sūrah, xxxiii
Idrîs, xxiv
Ignorance, Epoch of, xxii
'Isa, xxiii
Isaac, 66, 67
Isaiah, v, xi
Isḥâḳ, Abu, xv
Ishmaelites, xxv
Islâm, vii, xiv, xx, xxi, xxii, xxv, xxxi, xlii
Islâm, Encyclopaedia of, xxxi
Islâmic, xi, xvi, xxiv, xxvi
Isnâd, xxvi
Išo'iahb, xiv
Israel, 50, 51
Israelite, xiv, xxviii, xxix
Israelites, xxvii
Isrâ'il, Bani, xii, 50, 51, 74, 75
'Itâbah, xvii

Jacob, 66, 67
Jacob of Edessa, xxviii
Jacob, Mar, v, viii
Jerome, St, ix
Jerusalem, xxv
Jesus, xxiii
Jewish, ix, xii, xiii, xxiii, xxiv
Jews, xiv, xv, xxviii, xxix, 10, 11
John, xxiii
Joseph, xix
Joseph of Ahwâz, xxvii
Josephus, xiv
Judaeo-Christian, xxiv
Judaic, anti-, xxviii

Kadesia, xxv
Ḳâmūs, xxxvii
Ḳârḳaphta, xxviii
Ḳarūn, xxiv
Ḳatrian, xxx
Kefil, xxiv
Ḳennešrin, xxviii
Khalîl, Ibn Ahmad, xxix, xxxiii
Ḳiddušin, xxviii
Kisâ'i, xxix
Korah, xxiv
Kūfa, xxvii, xxix, xxx, xxxv
Kufi, xxxi
Kufic, vi
Kūfo-Naskhi, xxxi, xxxiii, xxxv
Ḳuraish, xi, xiii, xx
Kuraishites, xiii
Kurdish, xvii

Labourt, xxx
Latin, xxvi
Lees, Nassau, xxvi
Lewis, Dr Agnes Smith, xxxii, xlii
Lot, 66, 67
Luminous Book, xviii
Lyall, Sir Charles, xxii

Machriq, Al, xxx
Madâ'ini, xv
Maḥôzé, xxix
Mamo Ziné, xvii
Mandaeans, xxx
Mandaitic, xxx
Maracci, M., xxiv
Margaret, Maggie, Meg, Peggie, xxiii
Margoliouth, D. S., xx, xxi
Mariam, xxiv
Mary, the Virgin, xiv, 10, 11
Massorah, xxvii, xxix, xxxiv
Massoretic, xxix, xxxiv
Maswai, xxx
Mecca, xii, xiii, xv, xvi, xviii, xix, xxiv
Meccan, xiii
Medina, xvi, xix
Merx, M., xxviii
Mesopotomia, xvii, xxviii, xxix
Messiah, xiv, xxv, 10, 11
Mingana, Dr Alphonse, vi, vii, viii, ix, x, xiii, xxv, xxvi
Mira, xvii
Miriam, Mary, xiv, 10, 11
Monophysite, xxvii
Monophysites, xxviii
Moritz, B., xxxi
Moses, xiv, xxxv, 2, 3, 4, 5, 6, 7, 20, 21, 30, 31, 50, 51, 64, 65
Moslem, vii, ix, xi, xii, xviii, xxi, xxii, xxvi, 44, 45
Moslems, ix, x, xxi
Mu'âwiah, xxvii
Muḥammad, vii, xi, xii, xiii, xiv, xv, xvi, xvii, xviii, xx, xxi, xxiii, xxiv, xxv, xxvi, xxvii, xxix, xxxvii
Muḥammadan, xi, xii, xv, xvi, xviii, xxi, xxii, xxvii
Muḥammadanism, xi, xx, xxi, xxvi
Muḥammadans, xxi
Muir, Sir W., xxii
Mūsa, ibn 'Uqba, xv
Muslim, Abu, xxix
Musulmans, 44, 45

Nâbigha, xxii
Nakwergân, Ḳardagh, xiii
Narsai, xiii, xxviii
Naskhi, vi, xxxi
Nazarenes, 10, 11, 38, 39
Nehardea, xxix
Nestorian, xxviii, xxx, xxxi
Neubauer, xxviii
New Testament, x
Nicholson, R. A., xxx
Niebuhr, xxiv
Nile, xiv
Nisibis, xiii, xxviii
Noah, xxxv, 18, 19, 20, 21, 22, 23, 50, 51, 52, 53
Nöldeke, Dr, xii, xiii, xvi, xvii, xxii, xxvi, xxviii
Noun Agent, vi
Numbers, xxiv

Obadiah, xxiv
Old Latin, x
Old Testament, v, xxix
'Omar, xviii, xix, xxv
Oriental, vi
Orientalist, xxii

'Othmân, vii, xx, xxi, xxvii, xlii
'Othmânic, xxii
Oxford, v

Palaeographical Society, xxxi, xxxii
Palestine, xxviii
Palmer, E. H., xii
Paradise, the garden, 8, 9, 18, 19, 20, 21, 24, 25, 28, 29, 38, 39, 72, 73, 74
Parwez, xxx
Peleg, xxiv
Perozšabur, xxix
Persia, xiii, xxx
Persian, xiii, xxiv, xxvii, xxviii, xxx
Persians, xxviii
Pharaoh, xiv, 30, 31
Praised One, xxv
Pre-Islâmic, xxiii
Pre-'Othmânic, vii, x, xxii
Pre-Qurânic, xxxi
Preserved Table, xviii
Prophet (Muḥammad), vii, xi, xii, xiii, xiv, xv, xvi, xvii, xviii, xix, xx, xxi, xxii, xxiii, xxvi, xxvii, xl, 4, 5, 6, 7, 8, 9, 10, 11, 14, 15, 16, 17, 18, 19, 28, 29, 30, 31, 46, 47, 52, 53, 64, 65, 66, 67
Protevangelium Jacobi, v, viii, ix
Puḥâmés, xxvi, xxvii
Pumbaditha, xxix

Qurân (the Book), vi, viii, ix, x, xi, xii, xiii, xiv, xv, xvi, xvii, xviii, xix, xx, xxi, xxii, xxiii, xxv, xxvi, xxix, xxxii, xxxiii, xxxiv, xxxv, xxxvi, xxxvii, xxxviii, xxxix, xl, xlii, 28, 29, 32, 33, 42, 43, 44, 45, 50, 51, 58, 59, 61, 64, 65, 68, 69, 72, 73, 74
Qurânic, xi, xxxvii,

Rabbinic, xxix
Raḥmân, 'Abdur-, ibn Ormiz, xxvii
Robert, Bob, Bertie, xxiii
Rodwell, M., xxiv
Roman, ix, xiii, xxiv, xxviii

Sabrowy, Abba, xxviii
Sa'di, xxiv
Saffâḥ, xxvii
Sale, G., xviii
Ṣâleḥ, xxiv
Sanhedrin, xiv
Sapor I, xxviii
Sapor II, xxviii
Sassanide, xxviii, xxx
Sassanides xiii, xxiv, xxviii
Sassanido-Persians, xxviii
Satan, xvi, 44, 45, 54, 55, 60, 61, 62, 63
Saul, xiv, xxiv
Schechter, Dr Solomon, x
Sekkît, Ibn As-, xxix
Seleucia, xiii, xxix
Sell, E., xvi
Semitic, xxvi, xxvii, xxx
Shaharzūr, xxvii
Shakâki, xvii
Shammar, xvii
Shanfarâ, xxii
Shehak, Beth, xxviii
Shelah, xxiv
Shu'aib, xxiv
Sibawaihi, xxix
Sidra, xxviii
Sinai, Mount, v, xxiii
Sinaitic Syriac Version, xxxii, xlii
Sinaiticus, Cod., x
Son of God, 10, 11
Sora, xxviii
Spirit, Holy, xviii, 44, 45
Studia Sinaitica, v, vi, viii
Suez, v
Synodicon Orientale, xiii
Syria, viii, xiv, xvii
Syriac, v, ix, x, xxv, xxvii, xxviii, xxx, xxxi, xxxiv
Syriac Versions, x
Syrian, xiii, xxxiv
Syrians, xxviii, xxx

Ta'abbaṭa-Sharran, xxii
Ṭabari, xv, xx, xxvi, xxviii
Ṭagrît, xxvii
Talmud xxviii
Ṭalūt, xxiv
Ṭarafa, xxii
Ṭay, Ṭayayés, xiii
Ṭel'eda, xxviii
Terah, xxiv
Thamud, 18, 19, 61, 70, 71
Theodosius, v
Tiberian, xxix
Tippoo Sahib, Qurân, x
Tisdall, W. St Clair, xiii
Torah, xv, xxviii, xl, 4, 5
Transitus Mariae, v, viii
Ṭu'âites, xiii

Umayyad, xxv, xxvii

Vaticanus Cod., x
Vulgate, x

Wâḳidi, xv
Walîd, xxv
Wright, Dr W., xxxi

Yakût, xx
Yarmûk, xxv
Yathrîb, xix
Yoḥannan, xxiii

Zaid, ibn Thâbit, vii, xvii, xviii, xix, xx, xxi
Zamakhshari, Az-, xxvi
Zêwiki, xvii
Zobair, 'Abdallah ibn, xx
Zuhair, xxii
Zuhri, xv

نبذ ثمينة وقديمة
من القرآن الشريف

Fol. 59a

سورة ٧

v. 139 الجبل فان استقر مكنه فسوف تراني فلما تجلى ربه
v. 140 للجبل جعله دكا وخر موسى صعقا. فلما افق قل
v. 141 سبحنك تبت اليك وانا اول المومنين. قل يموسى
انى اصطفيتك على الناس برسلتي وبكلمي فخذ ما
v. 142 اتيتك وكن من الشكرين. وكتبنا له في الالوح من
كل شاي موعظة وتفصيلا لكل شاي فخذها بقوة و
امر قومك ياخذوا باحسنها ساريكم دار ا
v. 143 لفسقين. ساصرف عن ايتي الذين يتكبرون في الار
ض بغير الحق وان يروا كل اية لا يومنوا بها وان يروا
سبيل الرشد لا يتخذوه سبيلا وان يروا سبيل الغي
v. 144 يتخذوه سبيلا. ذلك بانهم كذبوا بايتنا وكا
v. 145 نوا عنها غفلين. والذين كذبوا بايتنا ولقا الاخر Fol. 54b
ة حبطت اعملهم هل يجزون الا ما كانوا يعملون.
v. 146 واتخذ قوم موسى من بعده من حليهم عجلا جسدا
له خوار الم يروا انه لا يكلمهم ولا يهديهمسبيلا
vv. 147–8 اتخذوه وكانوا ظلمين. ولما سقط في ايديهم و
راوا انهم قد ضلوا قالوا لين لم يرحمنا ربنا و
v. 149 يغفر لنا لنكونن من الخسرين. ولما رجع موسى الى قو
مه غضبن اسفا قل بيسما خلفتموني من بعدي ا
عجلتم امر ربكم والقى الالوح واخذ براس
اخيه يجره اليه قل ابن ام ان القوم استضعفوني و
كادوا يقتلونني فلا تشمت بي الاعدا ولا تجعلني مع
v. 150 القوم الظلمين. قل رب اغفر لي ولاخي واد

سورة ٧

v. ١٣٩ الجبل فإن استقرّ مكانه فسوف تراني فلمّا تجلّى ربّه
v. ١٤٠ للجبل جعله دكّا وخرّ موسى صعقا فلمّا أفاق قال
v. ١٤١ سبحانك تبت إليك وأنا أوّل المؤمنين قال يا موسى
إنّي اصطفيتك على النّاس برسالاتي وبكلامي فخذ ما
v. ١٤٢ آتيتك وكن من الشّاكرين وكتبنا له في الألواح من
كلّ شيء موعظة وتفصيلا لكلّ شيء فخذها بقوّة
وأمر قومك يأخذوا بأحسنها سأريكم دار
v. ١٤٣ الفاسقين سأصرف عن آياتي الّذين يتكبّرون في الأرض
بغير الحقّ وإن يروا كلّ آية لا يؤمنوا بها وإن يروا
سبيل الرّشد لا يتّخذوه سبيلا وإن يروا سبيل الغيّ
v. ١٤٤ يتّخذوه سبيلا ذلك بأنّهم كذّبوا بآياتنا وكانوا
v. ١٤٥ عنها غافلين والّذين كذّبوا بآياتنا ولقاء الآخرة
حبطت أعمالهم هل يجزون إلاّ ما كانوا يعملون
v. ١٤٦ واتّخذ قوم موسى من بعده من حليّهم عجلا جسدا
له خوار ألم يروا أنّه لا يكلّمهم ولا يهديهم سبيلا
vv. ١٤٧-٨ إتّخذوه وكانوا ظالمين ولمّا سقط في أيديهم
ورأوا أنّهم قد ضلّوا قالوا لئن لم يرحمنا ربّنا
v. ١٤٩ ويغفر لنا لنكوننّ من الخاسرين ولمّا رجع موسى إلى قومه
غضبان أسفا قال بئسما خلفتموني من بعدي
أعجلتم أمر ربّكم وألقى الألواح وأخذ برأس
أخيه يجرّه إليه قال ابن أمّ إنّ القوم استضعفوني
وكادوا يقتلونني فلا تشمت بي الأعداء ولا تجعلني مع
v. ١٥٠ القوم الظّالمين قال ربّ اغفر لي ولأخي وأد

Fol. 59 b

سورة ٧

vv. 150–1 خلنا في رحمتك وانت ارحم الرحمين. ان الذين ا
تخذوا العجل سينلهم غضب من ربهم وذلة في ا
v. 152 لحيوة الدنيا وكذلك نجزي المفترين. والذين عملوا ا
لسيت ثم تابوا من بعدها وامنوا ان ربك من بعدها
v. 153 لغفور رحيم. ولما سكت عن موسى الغضب اخذ
الالوح وفي نسختها هدى وسلم (?) للذين هم ل
v. 154 ربهم يرهبون. واختر موسى قومه سبعين رجلا لمقتنا
فلما اخذتهم الرجفة قل رب لو شت اهل
كتهم (?) من قبل وايي اتهلكنا بما فعل السفها منا
ان هي الا فتنتك تضل بها من تشا وتهدي من تشا انت
v. 155 ولينا فاغفر لنا وارحمنا وانت خير الغفرين. وا

Fol. 54 a . . . .

اليك قل عذبي اصيب به من اشا ورحمتي
وسعت كل شاي فساكتبها للذين يتقون ويوتون الز
v. 156 كوة والذين همبايتنا يومنون. الذين يتبعون الرسول ا
لنبي الامي الذي يجدونه مكتوبا عندهم في ال
تورة والانجيل يامرهم بالمعروف وينهم . . . .
. . . . و يحلّ لهم الطيبت ويحرم عليهم ا
لخبيث ويضع عنهم اصرهم والاغلل التي كانت
عليهم فالذين امنوا [[به (?) وعزروه (?) ونصروه (?)]] وا
تبعوا النور الذي انزل معه اوليك هم المفلحون
vv. 157–8 قل يا ايها الناس اني رسول الله اليكم جميعا. الذي
له [ملك السمو]ت والارض لا اله الا هو يحيي و

QURÂN C

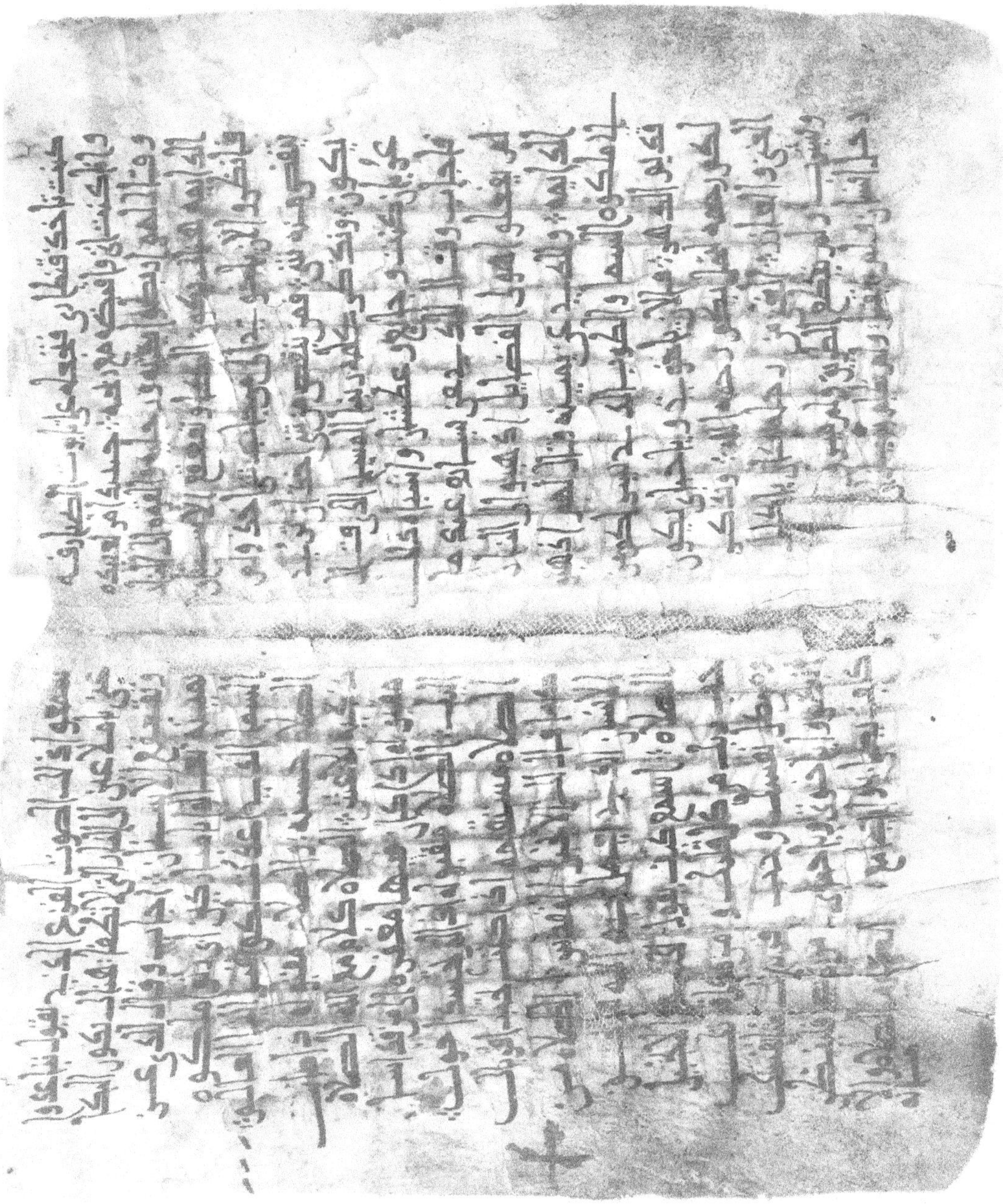

f. 59 b

f. 54 a

vv. ١٥٨—١٥٠ سورة ٧ Surah 7. *vv.* 150—158

سورة ٧

١٥٠-١ *vv.* خلنا في رحمتك وأنت أرحم الرّاحمين إنّ الّذين
اتّخذوا العجل سينالهم غضب من ربّهم وذلّة في
١٥٢ *v.* الحيوة الدنيا وكذلك نجزي المفترين والّذين عملوا
السّيّآت ثمّ تابوا من بعدها وآمنوا إنّ ربّك من بعدها
١٥٣ *v.* لغفور رحيم ولمّا سكت عن موسى الغضب أخذ
الألواح وفي نسختها هدى ورحمة للّذين هم
١٥٤ *v.* لربّهم يرهبون واختار موسى قومه سبعين رجلا لميقاتنا
فلمّا أخذتهم الرّجفة قال ربّ لو شئت أهلكتهم
من قبل وإيّاي أتهلكنا بما فعل السّفهآء منّا
إن هي إلّا فتنتك تضلّ بها من تشآء وتهدي من تشآء أنت
وليّنا فاغفر لنا وارحمنا وأنت خير الغافرين
١٥٥ *v.* واكتب لنا في هذه الدّنيا حسنة وفي الآخرة إنّا هدنا
إليك قال عذابي أصيب به من أشآء ورحمتي
وسعت كلّ شيء فسأكتبها للّذين يتّقون ويؤتون الزّكوة
١٥٦ *v.* والّذين هم بآياتنا يؤمنون الّذين يتّبعون الرّسول
النّبيّ الأمّيّ الّذي يجدونه مكتوبا عندهم في
التّوراة والإنجيل يأمرهم بالمعروف وينهاهم
عن المنكر ويحلّ لهم الطّيّبات ويحرّم عليهم
الخبآئث ويضع عنهم إصرهم والأغلال الّتي كانت
عليهم فالّذين آمنوا به وعزّروه ونصروه
واتّبعوا النّور الّذي أنزل معه أولآئك هم المفلحون
١٥٧-٨ *vv.* قل يا أيّها النّاس إنّي رسول اللّه إليكم جميعا ألّذي
له ملك السّموات والأرض لا إله إلّا هو يحيي

Fol. 103 a

سورة ٧

v. 158 يميت . . . . . النبي الامي الذي
يومن بالله وكلمته واتبعه لعلكم تهتدون

v. 159 ومن قوم موسى امة يهدون با . . وبه يعدلون

v. 160 قطع . . هم . . . . . اسباط . امما واوحينا الى
موسى اذ استسق . . قومه ان اضرب بعصاك

. . . .

. . . .

. . . .

وما ظلمونا ولكن كانوا انفسهم يظلمون

(النسخة تنقص نصف صحيفة)

. . . .

. . . .

v. 165 كانوا يفسقون . . . . Fol. 103b

. . . .

. . . .

. . . .

v. 168 . . . . يغفر لنا وان ياتهم عرض

. . . .

A. S. L.

سورة ٧

v. ١٥٨ ويميت فآمنوا بالله ورسوله النبيّ الأمّيّ الّذي
يؤمن بالله وكلماته واتّبعوه لعلّكم تهتدون

v. ١٥٩ ومن قوم موسى أمّة يهدون بالحقّ وبه يعدلون

v. ١٦٠ وقطّعناهم اثنتي عشرة أسباطا أمما وأوحينا إلى
موسى إذ استسقاه قومه أن اضرب بعصاك
الحجر فانبجست منه اثنتا عشرة عينا قد علم
كلّ أناس مشربهم وظلّلنا عليهم الغمام وأنزلنا
عليهم المنّ والسّلوى كلوا من طيّبات ما رزقناكم
وما ظلمونا ولكن كانوا أنفسهم يظلمون

vv.١٦٥-٦ كانوا يفسقون فلمّا عتوا عمّا نهوا عنه قلنا لهم
كونوا قردة خاسئين وإذ تأذّن ربّك ليبعثنّ
عليهم إلى يوم القيامة من يسومهم سوء العذاب
إنّ ربّك لسريع العقاب وإنّه لغفور رحيم

v. ١٦٧ وقطّعناهم في الأرض أمما منهم الصّالحون ومنهم
دون ذلك وبلوناهم بالحسنات والسّيّآت لعلّهم يرجعون

v. ١٦٨ فخلف من بعدهم خلف ورثوا الكتاب يأخذون عرض
هذا الأدنى ويقولون سيغفر لنا وإن يأتهم عرض
مثله يأخذوه ألم يؤخذ عليهم ميثاق الكتاب

Fol. 104 a

سورة ٩

vv. 18–19 اوليك ان يكونوا من المهتدين. اجعلتم سقية ا
لحج وعمرة المسجد الحرم كمن امن بالله واليوم
الاخر وجهد في سبيل الله لا يستون عند الله والله
v. 20 لا يهدي القوم الظلمين. الذين امنوا وهجروا وجهدو
ا في سبيل الله باموالهم وانفسهم اعظم درجة عند
v. 21 الله واوليك هم الفايزون. يبشرهم ربهم برحمة منه
v. 22 ورضون وجنات لهم فيها نعيم مقيم. خلدين فيها ابدا
v. 23 ان الله عنده اجر عظيم. يا ايها الذين امنوا لا تتخذوا
اباكم واخونكم اوليا ان استحبوا الكفر على الايمن فمن
v. 24 يتولهم منكم فاوليك هم الظلمون. قل ا . . .
. . . وكم واخونكم وا . . .
واموال اقترفتموها وتجـ . . .

Fol. 109 b

ضونها احب اليكم من الله ورسوله وجهد في
سبيله فتربصوا حتى ياتي الله بامره والله لا يهدا
v. 25 لقوم الفسقين. لقد نصركم الله في موطن كثيرة و
يوم حنين اذ اعجبتكم كثرتكم فلم تغن عنكم شيا وضا
قت عليكم الارض بما رحبت ثم وليتم مدبرين
v. 26 ثم انزل الله سكينته على رسوله وعلى المومنين وا
نزل جندا لم تروها وعذب الذين كفروا وذ
v. 27 لك جزا الكفرين. ثم يتوب الله من بعد ذلك
v. 28 على من يشا والله غفور رحيم. يا ايها الذين امنوا

سورة ٩

vv. ١٨-١٩ أولآئك أن يكونوا من المهتدين أجعلتم سقاية
الحاجّ وعمارة المسجد الحرام كمن آمن باللّه واليوم
الآخر وجاهد في سبيل اللّه لا يستوون عند اللّه واللّه
v. ٢٠ لا يهدي القوم الظّالمين ألّذين آمنوا وهاجروا وجاهدوا
في سبيل اللّه بأموالهم وأنفسهم أعظم درجة عند
v. ٢١ اللّه وأولآئك هم الفآئزون يبشّرهم ربّهم برحمة منه
v. ٢٢ ورضوان وجنّات لهم فيها نعيم مقيم خالدين فيها أبدا
v. ٢٣ إنّ اللّه عنده أجر عظيم يا أيّها الّذين آمنوا لا تتّخذوا
آبآءكم وإخوانكم أوليآء إن استحبّوا الكفر على الإيمان ومن
v. ٢٤ يتولّهم منكم فأولآئك هم الظّالمون قل إن كان آبآؤكم
وأبناؤكم وإخوانكم وأزواجكم وعشيرتكم
وأموال اقترفتموها وتجارة تخشون كسادها ومساكن
ترضونها أحبّ إليكم من اللّه ورسوله وجهاد في
سبيله فتربّصوا حتّى يأتي اللّه بأمره واللّه لا يهدي
v. ٢٥ القوم الفاسقين لقد نصركم اللّه في مواطن كثيرة
ويوم حنين إذ أعجبتكم كثرتكم فلم تغن عنكم شيئًا وضاقت
عليكم الأرض بما رحبت ثمّ ولّيتم مدبرين
v. ٢٦ ثمّ أنزل اللّه سكينته على رسوله وعلى المؤمنين
وأنزل جنودا لم تروها وعذّب الّذين كفروا
v. ٢٧ وذلك جزآء الكافرين ثمّ يتوب اللّه من بعد ذلك
v. ٢٨ على من يشآء واللّه غفور رحيم يا أيّها الّذين آمنوا

Fol. 104b

سورة ٩

v. 28 انما المشركون نجس فلا يقربوا المسجد الحرم بعد
عامهم هذا وان خفتم عيلة فسوف يغنيكم الله
v. 29 من فضله ان شا ان الله عليم حكيم. قتلوا الذين
لا يومنون بالله ولا باليوم الاخر ولا يحرمون ما حر
م الله ورسوله ولا يدينون دين الحق من الذين
اوتوا الكتب حتى يعطوا الجزية عن يد وهم
v. 30 صغرون. وقالت اليهود عزير ابن الله وقا
لت النصرى المسيح ابن الله ذلك قولهم
بافوههم يضهون قول الذين كفروا من قبل
v. 31 قتلهم الله انى يوفكون. اتخذوا احبرهم ور
. . . . دون الله والمسيح ابن . . وما

Fol. 109a . . . .

v. 32 عما يشركون. يريدون ان يطفوا نور الله بافو
ههم ويابى الله الا ان يتم نوره ولو كره الكفرون
v. 33 هو الذي ارسل رسوله بالهدى ودين الحق ليظهره
v. 34 على الدين كله ولو كره المشركون. يا ايها ا
لذين امنوا ان كثيرا من الاحبر والرهبن ليا كلو(!) ا
مول الناس بالبطل ويصدون عن سبيل الله وا
لذين يكنزون الذهب والفضة ولا ينفقونها
v. 35 في سبيل الله فبشرهم بعذاب اليم. يوم يحمى
عليها في نار جهنم فتكوى بها جبههم وجنو

سورة ٩

v. ٢٨ إنّما المشركون نجس فلا يقربوا المسجد الحرام بعد
عامهم هذا وإن خفتم عيلة فسوف يغنيكم اللّه
v. ٢٩ من فضله إن شآء إنّ اللّه عليم حكيم قاتلوا الّذين
لا يؤمنون باللّه ولا باليوم الآخر ولا يحرّمون ما حرّم
اللّه ورسوله ولا يدينون دين الحقّ من الّذين
أوتوا الكتاب حتّى يعطوا الجزية عن يد وهم
v. ٣٠ صاغرون وقالت اليهود عزير ابن اللّه وقالت
النّصارى المسيح ابن اللّه ذلك قولهم
بأفواههم يضاهئون قول الّذين كفروا من قبل
v. ٣١ قاتلهم اللّه أنّى يؤفكون إتّخذوا أحبارهم
ورهبانهم أربابا من دون اللّه والمسيح ابن مريم وما
أمروا إلّا ليعبدوا إلها واحدا لا إله إلّا هو سبحانه
v. ٣٢ عمّا يشركون يريدون أن يطفئوا نور اللّه بأفواههم
ويأبى اللّه إلّا أن يتمّ نوره ولو كره الكافرون
v. ٣٣ هو الّذي أرسل رسوله بالهدى ودين الحقّ ليظهره
v. ٣٤ على الدّين كلّه ولو كره المشركون يا أيّها
الّذين آمنوا إنّ كثيرا من الأحبار والرّهبان ليأكلون
أموال النّاس بالباطل ويصدّون عن سبيل اللّه
والّذين يكنزون الذّهب والفضّة ولا ينفقونها
v. ٣٥ في سبيل اللّه فبشّرهم بعذاب أليم يوم يحمى
عليها في نار جهنّم فتكوى بها جباههم

Fol. 60 a

سورة ٩

v. 35 بهم وظهورهم هذا ما كنزتم لانفسكم فذوقوا ما
v. 36 كنتم تكنزون. ان عدة الشهور عند الله اثنا عشر شهرا في
كتب الله يوم خلق السموت والارض منها اربعة حرم
ذلك الدين القيمفلا تظلموا فيها انفسكم وقتلوا المشركين
v. 37 كما يقتلونكم كافة واعلموا ان الله مع المتقين. انما ال
ناسي زيدة في الكفر يضل به الذين كفروا يحلون عا . . . .
ما . . . . . لهمسو اعملهم
v. 38 والله لا يهدا لقوم الكفرين. يا ايها الذين امنوا اذا قيل لكم
انفروا في سبيل الله . . . بالحيوة الدنيا من
v. 39 الاخرة فما متع الحيوة الدنيا في الاخرة الا قليل. الا تنفروا يعذبكم
عذبا اليما ويستبدل قوما غيركم ولا تضروه شيا والله على كل
Fol. 53 b . . . .
v. 40 اثنين اذ هما في الغار اذ يقول لصحبه لا تحزن ان الله معنا فانزل الله
سكينته عليه وايده بجنود لم تروها وجعل كلمة الذين كفروا
v. 41 السفلى وكلمة الله ⟦هي العليا والله عزيز حكيم؟⟧. انفروا خففا
وثقلا وجهدوا باmolكم وانفسكم في سبيل الله ⟦ ذلكم؟⟧ خير لكم
v. 42 ان كنتم تعلمون. لو كان عرضا قريبا وسفرا قصدا لاتبعوك
ولكن بعدت عليهم الشقة وسيحلفون بالله لو استطعنا
لخرجنا معكم يهلكون انفسهم والله يعلم انهم لكذبون
v. 43 عفا الله عنك لماذنت لهم حتى يتبين لك الذين صدقوا
v. 44 ومنهم الكذب⟦ون؟⟧. لا يستاذنك الذين يومنون بالله واليوم
الاخر ان يجهدوا باmolهم وانفسهم والله عليم بالمتقين.
v. 45 [انم]ا ي[ستاذنك] الذين لا يومنون بالله واليوم الاخر وار[تابت]

سورة ٩

v. ٣٥ وجنوبهم وظهورهم هذا ما كنزتم لأنفسكم فذوقوا ما
v. ٣٦ كنتم تكنزون إنّ عدّة الشّهور عند اللّه اثنا عشر شهرا في
كتاب اللّه يوم خلق السّموات والأرض منها أربعة حرم
ذلك الدّين القيّم فلا تظلموا فيهنّ أنفسكم وقاتلوا المشركين
v. ٣٧ كافّة كما يقاتلونكم كافّة واعلموا أنّ اللّه مع المتّقين إنّما
النّسيئ زيادة في الكفر يضلّ به الّذين كفروا يحلّونه عاما ويحرّمونه
عاما ليواطئوا عدّة ما حرّم اللّه فيحلّوا ما حرّم اللّه زيّن لهم سوّء أعمالهم
v. ٣٨ واللّه لا يهدي القوم الكافرين يا أيّها الّذين آمنوا ما لكم إذا قيل لكم
انفروا في سبيل اللّه إثّاقلتم إلى الأرض أرضيتم بالحيوة الدّنيا من
v. ٣٩ الآخرة فما متاع الحيوة الدّنيا في الآخرة إلّا قليل إلّا تنفروا يعذّبكم
عذابا أليما ويستبدل قوما غيركم ولا تضرّوه شيئًا واللّه على كلّ
v. ٤٠ شيء قدير إلّا تنصروه فقد نصره اللّه إذ أخرجه الّذين كفروا ثاني
اثنين إذ هما في الغار إذ يقول لصاحبه لا تحزن إنّ اللّه معنا فأنزل اللّه
سكينته عليه وأيّده بجنود لم تروها وجعل كلمة الّذين كفروا
v. ٤١ السّفلى وكلمة اللّه هي العليا واللّه عزيز حكيم إنفروا خفافا
وثقالا وجاهدوا بأموالكم وأنفسكم في سبيل اللّه ذلكم خير لكم
v. ٤٢ إن كنتم تعلمون لو كان عرضا قريبا وسفرا قاصدا لاتّبعوك
ولكن بعدت عليهم الشّقّة وسيحلفون باللّه لو استطعنا
لخرجنا معكم يهلكون أنفسهم واللّه يعلم إنّهم لكاذبون
v. ٤٣ عفا اللّه عنك لم أذنت لهم حتّى يتبيّن لك الّذين صدقوا
v. ٤٤ وتعلم الكاذبين لا يستأذنك الّذين يؤمنون باللّه واليوم
الآخر أن يجاهدوا بأموالهم وأنفسهم واللّه عليم بالمتّقين
v. ٤٥ إنّما يستأذنك الّذين لا يؤمنون باللّه واليوم الآخر وارتابت

Fol. 60 b

سورة ٩

vv. 45–46 قلوبهم فهم في ريبهم يترددون. ولو ارادوا الخروج لاعد
وا له عدة ولكن كره الله انبعٰثه[م فثبط]هم وقيل اقعدوا
v. 47 مع القعدين. لو خرجوا فيكم ما زادوكم الا خبلا ولاوضعو
ا خللكم يبغونكم الفتنة وفيكمسمعون لهم والله عليم با
v. 48 لظلمين. لقد ابتغوا الفتنة من قبل وقلبوا لك الامور حتى جا الحق
v. 49 وظهر امر الله وهم كرهون. ومنهم من يقول ايذن لي ولا [[تفتني]]؟
v. 50 الا في الفتنة سقطوا وان جهنم لمحيطة بالكفرين. ان تصبك حسنة
تسوهم وان تصبك مصيبة يقولوا قد اخذنا امرنا من قبل
v. 51 ويتولوا وهم فرحون. قل لن يصيبنا الا ما كتب الله لنا
v. 52 هو مولنا وعلى الله فليتوكل المومنون. قل هل تربصو
ن بنا الا احدى الحسنيين ونحن نتربص بكم ان يصيبكم الله

Fol. 53 a . . . .

v. 53 قل انفقوا طوعا او كرها لن يتقبل منكم انكم
v. 54 كنتم قوما فسقين. ما منعهم ان تقبل منهم نفقتهم الا
انهم كفروا بالله وبرسوله ولا ياتون الصلوة الا
v. 55 وهم كسلى ولا ينفقون الا وهم كرهون. فلا [[تعجبك]]؟ امو
لهم ولا اولدهم انما يريد الله ليعذبهم بها في الحيو
v. 56 ة الدنيا وتزهق انفسهم وهم كفرون. ويحلفون بالله انهم
v. 57 لمنكم وما هم منكم ولكنهم قوم يفرقون. لو يجدون
v. 58 ملجا او مغرت او مدخلا لولوا اليه وهم يجمحون. و
منهم من يلمزك في الصدقت فان اعطوا منها [[رضو]] (؟)
v. 59 ا وان لم يعطوا منها اذا هم يسخطون. ولو انهم رضو
ا ما اتهم الله ورسوله وقالوا حسبنا الله سيوتينا

سورة ٩

vv. ٤٥-٤٦ قلوبهم فهم في ريبهم يتردّدون ولو أرادوا الخروج لأعدّوا
له عدّة ولكن كره اللّه انبعاثهم فثبّطهم وقيل اقعدوا
v. ٤٧ مع القاعدين لو خرجوا فيكم ما زادوكم إلّا خبالا ولأوضعوا
خلالكم يبغونكم الفتنة وفيكم سمّاعون لهم واللّه عليم
v. ٤٨ بالظّالمين لقد ابتغوا الفتنة من قبل وقلّبوا لك الأمور حتّى جآء الحقّ
v. ٤٩ وظهر أمر اللّه وهم كارهون ومنهم من يقول ائذن لي ولا تفتنّي
v. ٥٠ ألا في الفتنة سقطوا وإنّ جهنّم لمحيطة بالكافرين إن تصبك حسنة
تسؤهم وإن تصبك مصيبة يقولوا قد أخذنا أمرنا من قبل
v. ٥١ ويتولّوا وهم فرحون قل لن يصيبنا إلّا ما كتب اللّه لنا
v. ٥٢ هو مولانا وعلى اللّه فليتوكّل المؤمنون قل هل تربّصون
بنا إلّا إحدى الحسنيين ونحن نتربّص بكم أن يصيبكم اللّه
بعذاب من عنده أو بأيدينا فتربّصوا إنّا معكم متربّصون
v. ٥٣ قل أنفقوا طوعا أو كرها لن يتقبّل منكم إنّكم
v. ٥٤ كنتم قوما فاسقين وما منعهم أن تقبل منهم نفقاتهم إلّا
أنّهم كفروا باللّه وبرسوله ولا يأتون الصّلوة إلّا
v. ٥٥ وهم كسالى ولا ينفقون إلّا وهم كارهون فلا تعجبك
أموالهم ولا أولادهم إنّما يريد اللّه ليعذّبهم بها في الحيوة
v. ٥٦ الدّنيا وتزهق أنفسهم وهم كافرون ويحلفون باللّه إنّهم
v. ٥٧ لمنكم وما هم منكم ولكنّهم قوم يفرقون لو يجدون
ملجأ أو مغارات أو مدّخلا لولّوا إليه وهم يجمحون
v. ٥٨ ومنهم من يلمزك في الصّدقات فإن أعطوا منها رضوا
v. ٥٩ وإن لم يعطوا منها إذا هم يسخطون ولو أنّهم رضوا
ما آتاهم اللّه ورسوله وقالوا حسبنا اللّه سيؤتينا

Fol. 105 a

سورة ٩

vv. 59–60 الله من فضله ورسوله انا الى الله رغبون. انما ا
لصدقت للفقرا والمسكين والعملين عليها والم[و]ا[فة]
قلوبهم وفي الرقاب والغرمين وفي سبيل الله وابن
v. 61 السبيل فريضة من الله والله عليم حكيم. ومنهم
الذين يوذون النبي ويقولون هو اذن قل اذن خير لكم يومن
v. 62 بالله ويومن للمومنين. ورحمة للذين امنوا منكم والذين
v. 63 يوذون رسول الله لهم عذب اليم. يحلفون بالله
لكم ليرضوكم والله ورسوله احق ان يرضوه ان
v. 64 كانوا مومنين. الم يعلموا انه من يحيدد الله ورسوله
v. 65 فان له نار جهنم خلدا فيها ذلك الخزي العظيم. يحذ
ر المنفقون ان تنزل عليهم سورة تنبيهم بما في قلوبهم قل
. . . ان الله مخرج ما تحذرون . . . .
v. 66 لن انما كنا نخوض ونلعب قل ابالله وايته ورسوله Fol. 108 b
v. 67 كنتم تستهزون. لا تعتذروا قد كفرتم بعد ايمنكم ان
نعف عن طايفة منكم نعذب طايفة بانهم كانوا
v. 68 مجرمين. المنفقون والمنفقات بعضهم من بعض يامرون
بالمنكر وينهون [عن المعروف ويقب]ضون ايديهم نسو
v. 69 الله فنسيهم [ان المنافقين هم] الفسقون. وعد الله ا
لمنفقين والمنفق[ات والكفار نار] جهنم خلدين فيها هي
v. 70 حسبهم ولعنهم [الله ولهم] عذب مقيم. كالذين
من قبلكم كانوا اشد منكم قوة واكثر امولا واو
لدا فاستمتعوا بخلقهم فاستمتعتم بخلقكم كما استمتع
الذين من قبلكم بخلقهم وخضتم كالذي خاضوا او

vv. ٥٩-٦٠ اللّه من فضله ورسوله إنّا إلى اللّه راغبون   إنّما

الصّدقات للفقراء والمساكين والعاملين عليها والمؤلّفة

قلوبهم وفي الرّقاب والغارمين وفي سبيل اللّه وابن

v. ٦١ السّبيل فريضة من اللّه واللّه عليم حكيم   ومنهم

الّذين يؤذون النّبيّ ويقولون هو أذن قل أذن خير لكم يؤمن

v. ٦٢ باللّه ويؤمن للمؤمنين   ورحمة للّذين آمنوا منكم والّذين

v. ٦٣ يؤذون رسول اللّه لهم عذاب أليم   يحلفون باللّه

لكم ليرضوكم واللّه ورسوله أحقّ أن يرضوه إن

v. ٦٤ كانوا مؤمنين   ألم يعلموا أنّه من يحادد اللّه ورسوله

v. ٦٥ فأنّ له نار جهنّم خالدا فيها ذلك الخزي العظيم   يحذر

المنافقون أن تنزّل عليهم سورة تنبّئهم بما في قلوبهم قل

v. ٦٦ استهزؤا إنّ اللّه مخرج ما تحذرون   ولئن سألتهم ليقولنّ

إنّما كنّا نخوض ونلعب قل أباللّه وآياته ورسوله

v. ٦٧ كنتم تستهزؤن   لا تعتذروا قد كفرتم بعد إيمانكم إن

نعف عن طائفة منكم نعذّب طائفة بأنّهم كانوا

v. ٦٨ مجرمين   المنافقون والمنافقات بعضهم من بعض يأمرون

بالمنكر وينهون عن المعروف ويقبضون أيديهم نسوا

v. ٦٩ اللّه فنسيهم إنّ المنافقين هم الفاسقون   وعد اللّه

المنافقين والمنافقات والكفّار نار جهنم خالدين فيها هي

v. ٧٠ حسبهم ولعنهم اللّه ولهم عذاب مقيم   كالّذين

من قبلكم كانوا أشدّ منكم قوّة وأكثر أموالا وأولادا

فاستمتعوا بخلاقهم فاستمتعتم بخلاقكم كما استمتع

الّذين من قبلكم بخلاقهم وخضتم كالّذي خاضوا

Fol. 105 b

سورة ٩

v. 70 ليك حبطت اعملهم في الدنيا والاخرة واو
v. 71 ليك هم الخسرون. الم ياتهم نبا الذين من قبلهم قوم
نوح وعاد وثمود وقوم ابرهيم واصحب مدين وا
لموتفكت اتتهم رسلهم بالبينت فما كان الله ليظلمهم
v. 72 ولكن كانوا انفسهم يظلمون. والمومنون والمومنت
بعضهم اوليا بعض يامرون بالمعروف وينهون عن المنك
ر ويقيمون الصيلوة (!) ويوتون الزكوة ويطيعون الله و
رسوله اوليك سيرحمهم الله ان الله عزيز حكيم.
v. 73 وعد الله المومنين والمومنت جنت تجري من
تحتها الانهر خلدين فيها ومسكن طيبة . . .
. . . ورضون من الله اكبر ذلك هو الفوز ا . . .
v. 74 . . . جهد الكفار والمنفقين [واغ]لظ
v. 75 عليهم وماوهم جهنم وبيس المصير. يحلفون با Fol. 108 a
لله ما قالوا ولقد قالوا كلمة الكفر وكفر
وا بعد اسلمهم وهموا بما لم ينللوا (!) وما نقموا
الا ان اغنهم الله ورسوله من فضله فان يتوبوا
يك خيرا لهم [وان يتولوا] يعذبهم [الله] عذابا ا
ليما في الدنيا والاخرة [وما لهم في] الارض من ولي
v. 76 ولا نصير. ومنهم من عهد [الله لئن] اتنا من فضله
v. 77 لنصدقن ولنكونن من الص[لحين. فلم]ا اتهم من فضله
v. 78 بخلوا به وتولوا وهم معرضون. فاعقبهم نفقا في
قلوبهم الى يوم يلقونه بما اخلفوا الله ما و
v. 79 عدوه وبما كانوا يكذبون. الم يعلموا ان الله

سورة ٩

v. ٧٠ أولآئك حبطت أعمالهم في الدّنيا والآخرة
v. ٧١ وأولآئك هم الخاسرون ألم يأتهم نبأ الّذين من قبلهم قوم
نوح وعاد وثمود وقوم إبرهيم وأصحاب مدين
والمؤتفكات أتتهم رسلهم بالبيّنات فما كان اللّه ليظلمهم
v. ٧٢ ولكن كانوا أنفسهم يظلمون والمؤمنون والمؤمنات
بعضهم اوليآء بعض يأمرون بالمعروف وينهون عن المنكر
ويقيمون الصّلوة ويؤتون الزّكوة ويطيعون اللّه
ورسوله أولآئك سيرحمهم اللّه إنّ اللّه عزيز حكيم
v. ٧٣ وعد اللّه المؤمنين والمؤمنات جنّات تجري من
تحتها الأنهار خالدين فيها ومساكن طيّبة في جنّات
عدن ورضوان من اللّه أكبر ذلك هو الفوز العظيم
v. ٧٤ يا أيّها النّبيّ جاهد الكفّار والمنافقين واغلظ
v. ٧٥ عليهم ومأواهم جهنّم وبئس المصير يحلفون
باللّه ما قالوا ولقد قالوا كلمة الكفر وكفروا
بعد إسلامهم وهمّوا بما لم ينالوا وما نقموا
إلّا أن أغناهم اللّه ورسوله من فضله فإن يتوبوا
يك خيرا لهم وإن يتولّوا يعذّبهم اللّه عذابا
أليما في الدّنيا والآخرة وما لهم في الأرض من وليّ
v. ٧٦ ولا نصير ومنهم من عاهد اللّه لئن آتانا من فضله
v. ٧٧ لنصّدّقنّ ولنكوننّ من الصّالحين فلمّا آتاهم من فضله
v. ٧٨ بخلوا به وتولّوا وهم معرضون فأعقبهم نفاقا في
قلوبهم إلى يوم يلقونه بما أخلفوا اللّه ما
v. ٧٩ وعدوه وبما كانوا يكذبون ألم يعلموا أنّ اللّه

Fol. 106 a

سورة ١١
v. 20 شهد منه ومن قبله كتاب موسى اماما ور
حمة اوليك يومنون به ومن يكفر به من الا
حزب فالنار موعده فلا تك في ⟦مرية⟧ (?) منه
انه الحق من ربك ولكن اكثر الناس لا يومنون
v. 21 ومن اظلم ممن افترى على الله كذبا اوليك
يعرضون على ربهم ويقول الاشهد هولا الذ
ين كذبوا على ربهم الا لعنة الله على ا
v. 22 لظلمين. الذين يصدون عن سبيل ⟦الله⟧ (?) ويبغو
نها عوجا وهم بالاخرة هم كفرون اوليك
لم يكونوا معجزين في الارض وما كان لهم من
دون الله من اوليا يضعف لهم العذاب

Fol 107 b . . . .

v. 23 اوليك الذين خسروا انفسهم وضل عنهم
v. 24 ما كانوا يفترون. لا جرم انهم في الاخرة هم
v. 25 لخسرون. ان الذين امنوا وعملوا الصلحت
وخبتوا الى ربهم اوليك اصحب الجنة
v. 26 هم فيها خلدون. مثل الفريقين كالاعمى والا
صم والبصير والسميع هل يستويان مثلا افلا
v. 27 تذكرون. ولقد ارسلنا نوحا الى قومه اني
v. 28 لكم [ن]ذير مبين. الا تعبدوا الا الله اني ا
v. 29 خاف عليكم عذاب يوم اليم. فقل
الملا الذين كفروا من قومه ما نراك الا
بشرا مثلنا وما نراك اتبعك الا الذين

سورة ١١

v. ٢٠ شاهد منه ومن قبله كتاب موسى إماما
ورحمة أولآئك يؤمنون به ومن يكفر به من
الأحزاب فالنّار موعده فلا تك في مرية منه
إنّه الحقّ من ربّك ولكنّ أكثر النّاس لا يؤمنون
v. ٢١ ومن أظلم ممّن افترى على اللّه كذبا أولآئك
يعرضون على ربّهم ويقول الأشهاد هؤلآء
الّذين كذبوا على ربّهم ألا لعنة اللّه على
v. ٢٢ الظّالمين الّذين يصدّون عن سبيل اللّه ويبغونها
عوجا وهم بالآخرة هم كافرون أولآئك
لم يكونوا معجزين في الأرض وما كان لهم من
دون اللّه من أوليآء يضاعف لهم العذاب
ما كانوا يستطيعون السّمع وما كانوا يبصرون
v. ٢٣ أولآئك الّذين خسروا أنفسهم وضلّ عنهم
v. ٢٤ ما كانوا يفترون لا جرم أنّهم في الآخرة هم
v. ٢٥ الأخسرون إنّ الّذين آمنوا وعملوا الصّالحات
وأخبتوا إلى ربّهم أولآئك أصحاب الجنّة
v. ٢٦ هم فيها خالدون مثل الفريقين كالأعمى والأصمّ
والبصير والسّميع هل يستويان مثلا أفلا
v. ٢٧ تذكّرون ولقد أرسلنا نوحا إلى قومه إنّي
v. ٢٨ لكم نذير مبين ألّا تعبدوا إلّا اللّه إنّي
v. ٢٩ أخاف عليكم عذاب يوم أليم فقال
الملأ الّذين كفروا من قومه ما نراك إلّا
بشرا مثلنا وما نراك اتّبعك إلّا الّذين

Fol. 106 b

سورة ١١

v. 29 هم ارذلنا بادي الراي وما نرى لكم
v. 30 علينا من فضل بل نظنكم كذبين. قل يقو
م اريتم ان كنت على بينة من ربي واتاني ر
حمة من عنده فعميت عليكم انلزمكموها
v. 31 وانتم لها كرهون. ويقوم لا اسلكم
عليه ملا ان اجري الا على الله وما انا بطر
د الذين امنوا انهم ملقوا ربهم ولكني اريكم
v. 32 قوما تجهلون. ويقوم من ينصرني من الله ان
v. 33 طردتهم افلا تذكرون. ولا اقول لكم
عندي خزاين الله ولا اعلم الغيب ولا
اقول اني ملك ولا اقول للذين تزدري [اع]
Fol. 107 a ينكم لن يوتيهم الله خيرا الله اعلم بما
v. 34 في انفسهم اني اذا لمن الظلمين. قلوا ينوح
قد جدلت فاكثرت جدلنا فاتنا بما تعد
v. 35 نا ان كنت من الصدقين. قل انما ياتيكم
v. 36 به الله ان شا وما انتم بمعجزين. ولا ينفعكم
نصحي ان اردت ان انصح لكم ان
كان الله يريد ان يغويكم هو ربكم وا
v. 37 ليه ترجعون. ام يقولون افتريه قل ان افتر
v. 38 يته [فعل]ي اج[رامي] وانا بري مما تجرمون. واو
حي الى نوح انه لن يومن من ق[وم]ك الا
v. 39 من قد امن فلا [تبتئ]س [بم]ا كانوا يفعلون. و
اصنع الفلك باعيننا ووحينا ولا تخطبني

سورة ١١
v. ٢٩ هم أراذلنا بادي الرّأي وما نرى لكم
v. ٣٠ علينا من فضل بل نظنّكم كاذبين قال يا قوم
أرأيتم إن كنت على بيّنة من ربّي وآتاني
رحمة من عنده فعمّيت عليكم أنلزمكموها
v. ٣١ وأنتم لها كارهون ويا قوم لا أسألكم
عليه مالا إن أجري إلّا على اللّه وما أنا بطارد
الّذين آمنوا إنّهم ملاقوا ربّهم ولكنّي أراكم
v. ٣٢ قوما تجهلون ويا قوم من ينصرني من اللّه إن
v. ٣٣ طردتهم أفلا تذكّرون ولا أقول لكم
عندي خزائن اللّه ولا أعلم الغيب ولا
أقول إنّي ملك ولا أقول للّذين تزدري
أعينكم لن يؤتيهم اللّه خيرا أللّه أعلم بما
v. ٣٤ في أنفسهم إنّي إذا لمن الظّالمين قالوا يا نوح
قد جادلتنا فأكثرت جدالنا فأتنا بما تعدنا
v. ٣٥ إن كنت من الصّادقين قال إنّما يأتيكم
v. ٣٦ به اللّه إن شآء وما أنتم بمعجزين ولا ينفعكم
نصحي إن أردت أن أنصح لكم إن
كان اللّه يريد أن يغويكم هو ربّكم
v. ٣٧ وإليه ترجعون أم يقولون افتراه قل إن افتريته
v. ٣٨ فعليّ إجرامي وأنا بريء ممّا تجرمون وأوحي
إلى نوح أنّه لن يؤمن من قومك إلّا
من قد آمن فلا تبتئس بما كانوا يفعلون
v. ٣٩ واصنع الفلك بأعيننا ووحينا ولا تخاطبني

Fol. 17 a

سورة ١٣

v. 18 استجبوا لربهم الحسنى والذين لم يستجيبوا له لو ان
لهم ما في الارض جميعا ومثله معه لافتدوا به
اوليك لهم سو الحسب وماوهم جهنم
v. 19 وبيس المهد. افمن يعلم انما انزل اليك من
ربك الحق كمن هو اعمى انما يتذكر اولو
v. 20 الالبب. الذين يوفون بعهد الله ولا
v. 21 ينقضون الميثق. والذين يصلون ما امر الله
به ان يوصل ويخشون ربهم ويخفون سو الحسا
v. 22 ب. والذين صبروا ابتغا وجه ربهم وا
قموا الصلوة وانفقوا مما رزقناهم سرا
Fol. 16 b وعلنية ويدرون بالحسنة السية اوليك
v. 23 لهم عقبى الدار. جنت عدن يدخلونها
ومن صلح من ابايهم وازوجهم وذريتهم
v. 24 والمليكة يدخلون عليهم من كل باب. سلم
v. 25 عليكم بما صبرتم فنعم عقبى الدار. والذ
ين ينقضون عهد الله من بعد ميثقه ويقطعون
ما امر الله به ان يوصل ويفسدون في الار
ض اوليك لهم اللعنة ولهم سو الدار
v. 26 والله يبسط الرزق لمن يشا ويقدر وفر
حوا بالحيوة الدنيا وما الحيوة الدنيا في
v. 27 الاخرة الا متاع. ويقول الذين كفروا لولا انزل

سورة ١٣

١٨ .v استجابوا لربّهم الحسنى والّذين لم يستجيبوا له لو أنّ
لهم ما في الأرض جميعا ومثله معه لافتدوا به
أولآئك لهم سوٓء الحساب ومأواهم جهنّم
١٩ .v وبئس المهاد أفمن يعلم أنّما أنزل إليك من
ربّك الحقّ كمن هو أعمى إنّما يتذكّر أولوا
٢٠ .v الألباب الّذين يوفون بعهد اللّه ولا
٢١ .v ينقضون الميثاق والّذين يصلون ما أمر اللّه
به أن يوصل ويخشون ربّهم ويخافون سوٓء الحساب
٢٢ .v والّذين صبروا ابتغآء وجه ربّهم
وأقاموا الصّلوة وأنفقوا مما رزقناهم سرّا
وعلانية ويدرؤن بالحسنة السّيّئة أولآئك
٢٣ .v لهم عقبى الدّار جنّات عدن يدخلونها
ومن صلح من آبآئهم وأزواجهم وذرّيّاتهم
٢٤ .v والملآئكة يدخلون عليهم من كلّ باب سلام
٢٥ .v عليكم بما صبرتم فنعم عقبى الدّار والّذين
ينقضون عهد اللّه من بعد ميثاقه ويقطعون
ما أمر اللّه به أن يوصل ويفسدون في الأرض
أولآئك لهم اللّعنة ولهم سوٓء الدّار
٢٦ .v أللّه يبسط الرّزق لمن يشآء ويقدر وفرحوا
بالحيوة الدّنيا وما الحيوة الدّنيا في
٢٧ .v الآخرة إلّا متاع ويقول الّذين كفروا لولا أنزل

Fol. 17 b

سورة ١٣

v. 27 عليه اية من ربه قل ان الله يضل من يشا ويهدي
v. 28 اليه من اناب. الذين امنوا وتطمن قلوبهم
بذكر الله الا بذكر الله تطمن القلوب
الذين امنوا وعملوا الصلحت طوبى لهم
v. 29 وحسن ماب. كذلك ارسلنك في امة
قد خلت من قبلها امم لتتلوا (!) عليهم الذي او
حينا اليك وهم يكفرون بالرحمن قل هو ربي
لا اله الا هو عليه توكلت واليه متاب
v. 30 ولو ان قرنا سيرت به الجبل او قطعت به
الارض او كلم به الموتى بل لله الامر جميعا
Fol. 16 a افلم ييس الذين امنوا ان لو يشا الله لهدى
v. 31 الناس جميعا. ولا يزل الذين كفروا تصيبهم
بما صنعوا قارعة او تحل قريبا من دارهم حتى
ياتي وعد الله ان الله لا يخلف الميعد
v. 32 ولقد استهزي برسل من قبلك فامليت للذ
ين كفروا ثم اخذتهم فكيف كان عقاب
v. 33 افمن هو قيم على كل نفس بما كسبت وجعلو
ا لله شركا قل سموهم ام تنبونه بما لا ⟦يعلم⟧ (?)
في الارض ام بظاهر من القول بل فزين للذين
كفروا مكرهم وصدوا عن السبيل ومن يضلل
v. 34 الله فما له من هاد. لهم عذاب في الحيوة

سورة ١٣

v. ٢٧ عليه آية من ربّه قل إنّ اللّه يضلّ من يشآء ويهدي
v. ٢٨ إليه من أناب الّذين آمنوا وتطمئنّ قلوبهم
بذكر اللّه ألا بذكر اللّه تطمئنّ القلوب
ألّذين آمنوا وعملوا الصّالحات طوبى لهم
v. ٢٩ وحسن مآب كذلك أرسلناك في أمّة
قد خلت من قبلها أمم لتتلو عليهم الّذي
أوحينا إليك وهم يكفرون بالرّحمن قل هو ربّي
لا إله إلّا هو عليه توكّلت وإليه متاب
v. ٣٠ ولو أنّ قرآنا سيّرت به الجبال أو قطّعت به
الأرض أو كلّم به الموتى بل للّه الأمر جميعا
أفلم ييأس الّذين آمنوا أن لو يشآء اللّه لهدى
v. ٣١ النّاس جميعا ولا يزال الّذين كفروا تصيبهم
بما صنعوا قارعة أو تحلّ قريبا من دارهم حتّى
يأتي وعد اللّه إنّ اللّه لا يخلف الميعاد
v. ٣٢ ولقد استهزئ برسل من قبلك فأمليت للّذين
كفروا ثمّ أخذتّهم فكيف كان عقاب
v. ٣٣ أفمن هو قآئم على كلّ نفس بما كسبت وجعلوا
للّه شركآء قل سمّوهم أم تنبّئونه بما لا يعلم
في الأرض أم بظاهر من القول بل زيّن للّذين
كفروا مكرهم وصدّوا عن السّبيل ومن يضلل
v. ٣٤ اللّه فما له من هاد لهم عذاب في الحيوة

Fol. 19 a

سورة ١٣

v. 34 الدنيا ولعذاب الاخرة اشق وما لهم من الله
v. 35 من واق. مثل الجنة التي وعد المتقون تجري من تحتها
الانهر اكلها دايم وظلها تلك عقبى الذين ا
v. 36 تقوا وعقبى الكفرين النار. والذين اتينهم الكتب
يفرحون بما انزل اليك ومن الاحزب من ينكر
بعضه قل انما امرت ان اعبد الله ولا اش
v. 37 رك به اليه ادعو واليه ماب. وكذلك
انزلنه حكما عربيا ولين اتبعت اهواهم بعد
ما جاك من العلم ما لك من الله من ولي ولا
v. 38 واق. ولقد ارسلنا رسلا من قبلك وجعلنا
لهم ازوجا وذرية وما كان لرسول ان ياتي با Fol. 14 b
v. 39 ية الا باذن الله لكل اجل كتب. يمحوا (!) الله
v. 40 ما يشا [ويثبت] وعنده ام الكتب. وان ما (!) نرينك
بعض [الذي] نعدهم او نتوفينك فانما عليك
v. 41 البلغ [وعلينا] الحساب. [اولم يروا] انا ناتي ا
لارض ننقصها من اطرفها والله يحكم لا
v. 42 مع[قب] ل[حكـ]ـمه وهو سريع الحساب. وقد مكر
الذين من قبلهم فلله المكر جميعا يعلم ما تكسب
v. 43 كل نفس وسيعلم الكفر لمن عقبى الدار. ويقول
الذين كفروا لست مرسلا قل كفى بالله
شهيدا بيني وبينـ[ـكم] ومن عنده عيلم (!) الكتب

سورة ١٣
v. ٣٤ الدّنيا ولعذاب الآخرة أشقّ وما لهم من الله
v. ٣٥ من واق مثل الجنّة الّتي وعد المتّقون تجري من تحتها
الأنهار أكلها دآئم وظلّها تلك عقبى الّذين
v. ٣٦ اتّقوا وعقبى الكافرين النّار والّذين آتيناهم الكتاب
يفرحون بما أنزل إليك ومن الأحزاب من ينكر
بعضه قل إنّما أمرت أن أعبد الله ولا
v. ٣٧ أشرك به إليه أدعو وإليه مآب وكذلك
أنزلناه حكما عربيّا ولئن اتّبعت أهوآءهم بعد
ما جآءك من العلم ما لك من الله من وليّ ولا
v. ٣٨ واق ولقد أرسلنا رسلا من قبلك وجعلنا
لهم أزواجا وذرّيّة وما كان لرسول أن يأتي
v. ٣٩ بآية إلّا بإذن الله لكلّ أجل كتاب يمحو الله
v. ٤٠ ما يشآء ويثبت وعنده أمّ الكتاب وإمّا نرينّك
بعض الّذي نعدهم أو نتوفّينّك فإنّما عليك
v. ٤١ البلاغ وعلينا الحساب أولم يروا أنّا نأتي
الأرض ننقصها من أطرافها والله يحكم لا
v. ٤٢ معقّب لحكمه وهو سريع الحساب وقد مكر
الّذين من قبلهم فللّه المكر جميعا يعلم ما تكسب
v. ٤٣ كلّ نفس وسيعلم الكفّار لمن عقبى الدّار ويقول
الّذين كفروا لست مرسلا قل كفى بالله
شهيدا بيني وبينكم ومن عنده علم الكتاب

Fol. 19 b

سورة ١٤

v. 1 بسم الله الرحمن الرحيم الر ك[تا]ب انزلنه ا
ليك لتخرج الناس من [الظلمات] الى النور
v. 2 باذن ربهم الى صرط العزيز الحميد. الله ا
لذي له ما في السموت وما في [الارض] وويل
v. 3 للكفرين من عذاب شديد. الذين يستحبو
ن الحيوة الدنيا على الاخ[رة وي]صدون عن
سبيل الله ويبغونها عوجا اوليك في ضل
v. 4 بعيد. وما ارسلنا من رسول الا [بلسان] قومه
ليبين لهم فيضل الله من يشا ويهدي من يشا و Fol. 14 a
v. 5 هو العزيز الحكيم. ولقد ارسلنا موسى با
يتنا ان اخرج قومك من الظلمت الى
النور وذكرهم بايم الله ان في ذلك لايت
v. 6 لكل ص[بار] شك[ور]. واذ قال موسى لقومه ا
ذكروا نعمة الله عليكم اذ انجكم من ال
فرعون يسومونكم سو العذاب و[يذبح]ون
ابناكم ويستحيون نساكم وفي ذلكم بلا من
v. 7 ربكم عظيم. واذ تاذن ربكم لين شكرتم لازيد
v. 8 نكم ولين كفرتم ان عذابي لشديد. وقال موسى
ان تكفروا انتم ومن في الا[رض] جميعا فان الله

سورة ١٤

v. ١ بسم الله الرّحمن الرّحيم الّر كتاب أنزلناه
إليك لتخرج النّاس من الظّلمات إلى النّور
v. ٢ بإذن ربّهم إلى صراط العزيز الحميد الله
الّذي له ما في السّموات وما في الأرض وويل
v. ٣ للكافرين من عذاب شديد الّذين يستحبّون
الحيوة الدّنيا على الآخرة ويصدّون عن
سبيل الله ويبغونها عوجا أولآئك في ضلال
v. ٤ بعيد وما أرسلنا من رسول إلّا بلسان قومه
ليبيّن لهم فيضلّ الله من يشآء ويهدي من يشآء
v. ٥ وهو العزيز الحكيم ولقد أرسلنا موسى
بآياتنا أن أخرج قومك من الظّلمات إلى
النّور وذكّرهم بأيّام الله إنّ في ذلك لآيات
v. ٦ لكلّ صبّار شكور وإذ قال موسى لقومه
اذكروا نعمة الله عليكم إذ أنجاكم من آل
فرعون يسومونكم سوٓء العذاب ويذبّحون
أبنآءكم ويستحيون نسآءكم وفي ذلكم بلآء من
v. ٧ ربّكم عظيم وإذ تأذّن ربّكم لئن شكرتم لأزيدنّكم
v. ٨ ولئن كفرتم إنّ عذابي لشديد وقال موسى
إن تكفروا أنتم ومن في الأرض جميعا فإنّ الله

Fol. 18 a

سورة ١٥

v. 85 وما بينهما الا بالحق وان الساعة لاتية فا
v. 86 صفح الصفح الجميل. ان ربك هو الخلق
v. 87 العليم. ولقد اتيناك سبعا من المثاني والقر
v. 88 ان العظيم. لا تمدن عينيك الى ما متعنا
به ازواجا منهم ولا تحزن عليهم واخفض
v. 89 جناحك للمومنين. وقل اني انا النذير
vv. 90–91 المبين. كما انزلنا على المقتسمين. الذين
v. 92 جعلوا القران عضن. فوربك لنسالنهم اجمعين.
vv. 93–94 عما كانوا يعملون. فاصدع بما تومر
v. 95 واعرض عن المشركين. انا كفينك ا
v. 96 لمستهزين. الذين يجعلون مع الله الها اخر
v. 97 فسوف يعلمون. ولقد نعلم انك يضيق
v. 98 صدرك بما يقولون. فسبح بحمد ربك Fol. 15 b
v. 99 وكن من السجدين. واعبد ربك حتى ياتيك اليقين

سورة ١٦

v. 1 بسم الله الرحمن الرحيم اتى امر الله
v. 2 فلا تستعجلوه سبحنه وتعلى عما يشركون. ينز
ل المليكة بالروح من امره على من يشا
من عباده ان انذروا انه لا اله الا انا فا
v. 3 تقون. خلق السموت والارض بالحق تعلى
v. 4 عما يشركون. خلق الانسن من نطفة فاذا هو

سورة ١٥
v. ٨٥ وما بينهما إلّا بالحقّ وإنّ السّاعة لآتية
v. ٨٦ فاصفح الصّفح الجميل إنّ ربّك هو الخلّاق
v. ٨٧ العليم ولقد آتيناك سبعا من المثاني والقرآن
v. ٨٨ العظيم لا تمدّنّ عينيك إلى ما متّعنا
به أزواجا منهم ولا تحزن عليهم واخفض
v. ٨٩ جناحك للمؤمنين وقل إنّي أنا النّذير
vv. ٩٠-٩١ المبين كما أنزلنا على المقتسمين الّذين
v. ٩٢ جعلوا القرآن عضين فوربّك لنسألنّهم أجمعين
vv. ٩٣-٩٤ عمّا كانوا يعملون فاصدع بما تؤمر
v. ٩٥ وأعرض عن المشركين إنّا كفيناك
v. ٩٦ المستهزئين الّذين يجعلون مع الله إلها آخر
v. ٩٧ فسوف يعلمون ولقد نعلم أنّك يضيق
v. ٩٨ صدرك بما يقولون فسبّح بحمد ربّك
v. ٩٩ وكن من السّاجدين واعبد ربّك حتى يأتيك اليقين

سورة ١٦
v. ١ بسم الله الرّحمن الرّحيم أتى أمر الله
v. ٢ فلا تستعجلوه سبحانه وتعالى عمّا يشركون ينزّل
الملآئكة بالرّوح من أمره على من يشآء
من عباده أن أنذروا أنّه لا إله إلّا أنا
v. ٣ فاتّقون خلق السّموات والأرض بالحقّ تعالى
v. ٤ عمّا يشركون خلق الإنسان من نطفة فإذا هو

Fol. 18 b

سورة ١٦

v. 5 خصيم مبين. والانعم خلقها لكم فيها دف
v. 6 ومنفع ومنها تاكلون. ولكم فيها جمل حين تريحو
v. 7 ن وحين تسرحون. ⟦وتحمل⟧ (?) اثقالكم الى بلد
لم تكونوا بالغيه الا بشق الانفس ان ربكم
v. 8 لروف رحيم. والخيل والبغال والحمير لتر
v. 9 كبوها وزينة ويخلق ما لا تعلمون. وعلى ا
لله قصد السبيل ومنها جار ولو شا لهد
v. 10 يكم اجمعين. هو الذي انزل من السما ما لكم
v. 11 منه شرب ومنه شجر فيه تسيمون. ينبت لكم
به الزرع والزيتون والنخيل والاعنب
ومن كل الثمرت ان في ذلك لاية لقوم
Fol. 15 a *v.* 12 يتفكرون. وسخر لكم الليل والنهر والشمس
والقمر والنجم مسخرت بامره ان في ذ
v. 13 لك لايت لقوم يعقلون. وما ذرا لكم
في الارض مختلفا الونه ان في ذلك لاية
v. 14 لقوم يذكرون. وهو الذي سخر البحر لتاكلو
ا منه لحما طريا وتستخرجوا منه حلية تلبسونها
وتر (!) الفلك موخر فيه ولتبتغوا من فضله
v. 15 ولعلكم تشكرون. والقى في الارض روسي
ان تميد بكم وانهرا وسبلا لعلكم تهتدو
vv. 16–17 ن. وعلامت وبالنجم هم يهتدون. افمن يخل
v. 18 ق كمن لا يخلق اولا تذكرون. وان تعدوا

سورة ١٦

v. ٥ خصيم مبين والأنعام خلقها لكم فيها دفء
v. ٦ ومنافع ومنها تأكلون ولكم فيها جمال حين تريحون
v. ٧ وحين تسرحون وتحمل أثقالكم إلى بلد
لم تكونوا بالغيه إلّا بشقّ الأنفس إنّ ربّكم
v. ٨ لرؤف رحيم والخيل والبغال والحمير
v. ٩ لتركبوها وزينة ويخلق ما لا تعلمون وعلى
اللّه قصد السّبيل ومنها جآئر ولو شآء لهداكم
v. ١٠ أجمعين هو الّذي أنزل من السّمآء مآء لكم
v. ١١ منه شراب ومنه شجر فيه تسيمون ينبت لكم
به الزّرع والزّيتون والنّخيل والأعناب
ومن كلّ الثّمرات إنّ في ذلك لآية لقوم
v. ١٢ يتفكّرون وسخّر لكم اللّيل والنّهار والشّمس
والقمر والنّجوم مسخّرات بأمره إنّ في
v. ١٣ ذلك لآيات لقوم يعقلون وما ذرأ لكم
في الأرض مختلفا ألوانه إنّ في ذلك لآية
v. ١٤ لقوم يذّكّرون وهو الّذي سخّر البحر لتأكلوا
منه لحما طريّا وتستخرجوا منه حلية تلبسونها
وترى الفلك مواخر فيه ولتبتغوا من فضله
v. ١٥ ولعلّكم تشكرون وألقى في الأرض رواسي
أن تميد بكم وأنهارا وسبلا لعلّكم تهتدون
vv. ١٦-١٧ وعلامات وبالنّجم هم يهتدون أفمن يخلق
v. ١٨ كمن لا يخلق أفلا تذكّرون وإن تعدّوا

Fol. 20a

سورة ١٦

v. 18 نعمة الله لا تحصوها ان الله لغفور رحيم
vv. 19–20 والله يعلم ما تسرون وما تعلنون. والذين
يدعون من دون الله لا يخلقون شيا وهم
vv. 21–22 يخلقون. اموت غير احيا وما يشعرون. اين
v. 23 يبعثون. الهكم اله وحد فالذين لا يومنون
v. 24 بالاخرة قلوبهم منكرة وهم مستكبرون. لا
v. 25 جرم ان الله يعلم ما تسرون وما يعلنون. انه لا
v. 26 يحب المستكبرين. واذا قيل لهم ما ذا ان
v. 27 زل ربكم قالوا اساطير الاولين. ليحملوا او
زرهم كملة يوم القيمة ومن اوزر الذين
v. 28 يضلونهم بغير علم الا سا ما يزرون. قد

Fol. 13b . . . .

عد فخر عليهم السقف من فوقهم واتيهم
v. 29 [العذاب] من حيث لا يشعرون. ثم يوم القيمة
يخزيهم ويقول اين شركاي الذين كنتم تشقون
فيهم قل الذين اوتوا العلم ان الخزي اليو
v. 30 م والسو على الكفرين. الذين تتوفيهم ا
لمليكة ظلمي انفسهم فالقوا السلم ما كنا
نعمل من سو بل ان الله عليم بما كنتم
v. 31 تعملون. فادخلوا ابوب جهنم خلدين
v. 32 فيها فلبيس مثوى المتكبرين. وقل للذين ا
تقوا ما ذا انزل ربكم [قالوا خيرا] للذين احسنوا

سورة ١٦

v. ١٨ نعمة اللّه لا تحصوها إنّ اللّه لغفور رحيم
vv. ١٩-٢٠ واللّه يعلم ما تسرّون وما تعلنون والّذين
يدعون من دون اللّه لا يخلقون شيئا وهم
vv. ٢١-٢٢ يخلقون أموات غير أحيآء وما يشعرون أيّان
v. ٢٣ يبعثون إلهكم إله واحد فالّذين لا يؤمنون
v. ٢٤ بالآخرة قلوبهم منكرة وهم مستكبرون لا
v. ٢٥ جرم أنّ اللّه يعلم ما يسرّون وما يعلنون إنّه لا
v. ٢٦ يحبّ المستكبرين وإذا قيل لهم ما ذا أنزل
v. ٢٧ ربّكم قالوا أساطير الأوّلين ليحملوا
أوزارهم كاملة يوم القيامة ومن أوزار الّذين
v. ٢٨ يضلّونهم بغير علم ألا سآء ما يزرون قد
مكر الّذين من قبلهم فأتى اللّه بنيانهم من القواعد
فخرّ عليهم السّقف من فوقهم وأتاهم
v. ٢٩ العذاب من حيث لا يشعرون ثمّ يوم القيامة
يخزيهم ويقول أين شركآءي الّذين كنتم تشاقّون
فيهم قال الّذين أوتوا العلم إنّ الخزي اليوم
v. ٣٠ والسّوٓء على الكافرين الّذين تتوفّاهم
الملآئكة ظالمي أنفسهم فألقوا السّلم ما كنّا
نعمل من سوٓء بلى إنّ اللّه عليم بما كنتم
v. ٣١ تعملون فادخلوا أبواب جهنّم خالدين
v. ٣٢ فيها فلبئس مثوى المتكبّرين وقيل للّذين
اتّقوا ما ذا أنزل ربّكم قالوا خيرا للّذين أحسنوا

Fol. 20b

سورة ١٦

v. 32 في هذه الدنيا حسنة ولدار الاخرة خير ولنعم
v. 33 دار المتقين. جنت عدن يدخلونها تجري من
تحتها الانهر لهم فيها ما يشاون كذلك
v. 34 يجزي الله المتقين. الذين تتوفيهم الملیكة
طيبين يقولون سلم عليكم ادخلوا الجنة بما
v. 35 كنتم تعملون. هل ينظرون الا ان تاتيهم الملیكة
او ياتي امر ربك كذلك فعل الذين من
قبلهم وما ظلمهم الله ولكن كانوا انفسهم
v. 36 يظلمون. فاصبتهم سيت ما عملوا وحاق بهم
v. 37 ما كانوا به يستهزون. وقل الذين اشركوا
لو شا الله ما عبدنا من دونه من شي نحن ولا
. . . .

Fol. 13a

الذين من قبلهم فهل على الرسل الا البلغ ا
v. 38 لمبين. ولقد بعثنا في كل امة رسولا ان ا
عبدوا الله واجتنبوا الطغوت فمنهم من
هدى الله ومنهم من حقت عليه الضللة
فسيروا في الارض وانظروا كيف كان
v. 39 عقبة المكذبين. ان تحرص على هديهم
فان الله لا يهدي من يضل وما لهم من نصر
v. 40 ين. واقسموا بالله جهد ايمنهم لا يبعث
الله من يموت [بلى] وعدا عليه حقا ولكن
v. 41 اكثر الناس [لا يعلمون]. ليبين لهم الذي يختلفون

سورة ١٦

v. ٣٢ في هذه الدّنيا حسنة ولدار الآخرة خير ولنعم

v. ٣٣ دار المتّقين جنّات عدن يدخلونها تجري من
تحتها الأنهار لهم فيها ما يشآؤن كذلك

v. ٣٤ يجزي اللّه المتّقين الّذين تتوفّاهم الملائكة
طيّبين يقولون سلام عليكم ادخلوا الجنّة بما

v. ٣٥ كنتم تعملون هل ينظرون إلّا أن تأتيهم الملائكة
أو يأتي أمر ربّك كذلك فعل الّذين من
قبلهم وما ظلمهم اللّه ولكن كانوا أنفسهم

v. ٣٦ يظلمون فأصابهم سيّآت ما عملوا وحاق بهم

v. ٣٧ ما كانوا به يستهزؤن وقال الّذين أشركوا
لو شآء اللّه ما عبدنا من دونه من شيء نحن ولا
آبآؤنا ولا حرّمنا من دونه من شيء كذلك فعل
الّذين من قبلهم فهل على الرّسل إلّا البلاغ

v. ٣٨ المبين ولقد بعثنا في كلّ أمّة رسولا أن
اعبدوا اللّه واجتنبوا الطّاغوت فمنهم من
هدى اللّه ومنهم من حقّت عليه الضّلالة
فسيروا في الأرض فانظروا كيف كان

v. ٣٩ عاقبة المكذّبين إن تحرص على هداهم
فإنّ اللّه لا يهدي من يضلّ وما لهم من ناصرين

v. ٤٠ وأقسموا باللّه جهد أيمانهم لا يبعث
اللّه من يموت بلى وعدا عليه حقّا ولكنّ

v. ٤١ أكثر النّاس لا يعلمون ليبيّن لهم الّذي يختلفون

Fol. 58 b

سورة ١٦

vv. 80–81 والافدة لعلكم تشكرون. الم يروا الى الطير
مسخرت في جو السما ما يمسكهن الا الله ا
v. 82 ن في ذلك لايت لقوم يومنون. والله
جعل لكم من بيوتكم سكنا وجعل لكم من
جلود الانعم بيوتا تستخفونها يوم ظعنكم
ويوم اقيمتكم ومن اصوفها واوبرها
v. 83 واشعرها اثثا ومتعا الى حين. والله جعل
لكم مما خلق ظللا وجعل لكم من الجبل ا
كننا وجعل لكم سربيل تقيكم الحر وسر
بيل تقيكم باسكم كذلك يتم نعمته
v. 84 عليكم لعلكم تسلمون. فان تولوا فانما
v. 85 عليك البلغ المبين. يعرفون نعمة الله Fol. 55 a
v. 86 ثم ينكرونها واكثرهم الكفرون. ويوم
نبعث من كل امة شهيدا ثم لا يوذن للذين
v. 87 كفروا ولا هم يستعتبون. واذ را (!) الذين
ظلموا العذاب فلا يخفف عنهم ولا
v. 88 هم ينظرون. واذ را (!) الذين اشركوا شر
كاهم قلوا ربنا هولا شركانا الذين كنا
ندعو من دونك فالقوا اليهم القول انكم لكذبون.
v. 89 والقوا الى الله يومذ السلم وضل عنهم ما كانوا يفترون.
v. 90 الذين كفروا وصدوا عن سبيل الله زدنهم عذا
با فوق العذاب بما كانوا يفسدون

f. 58 b

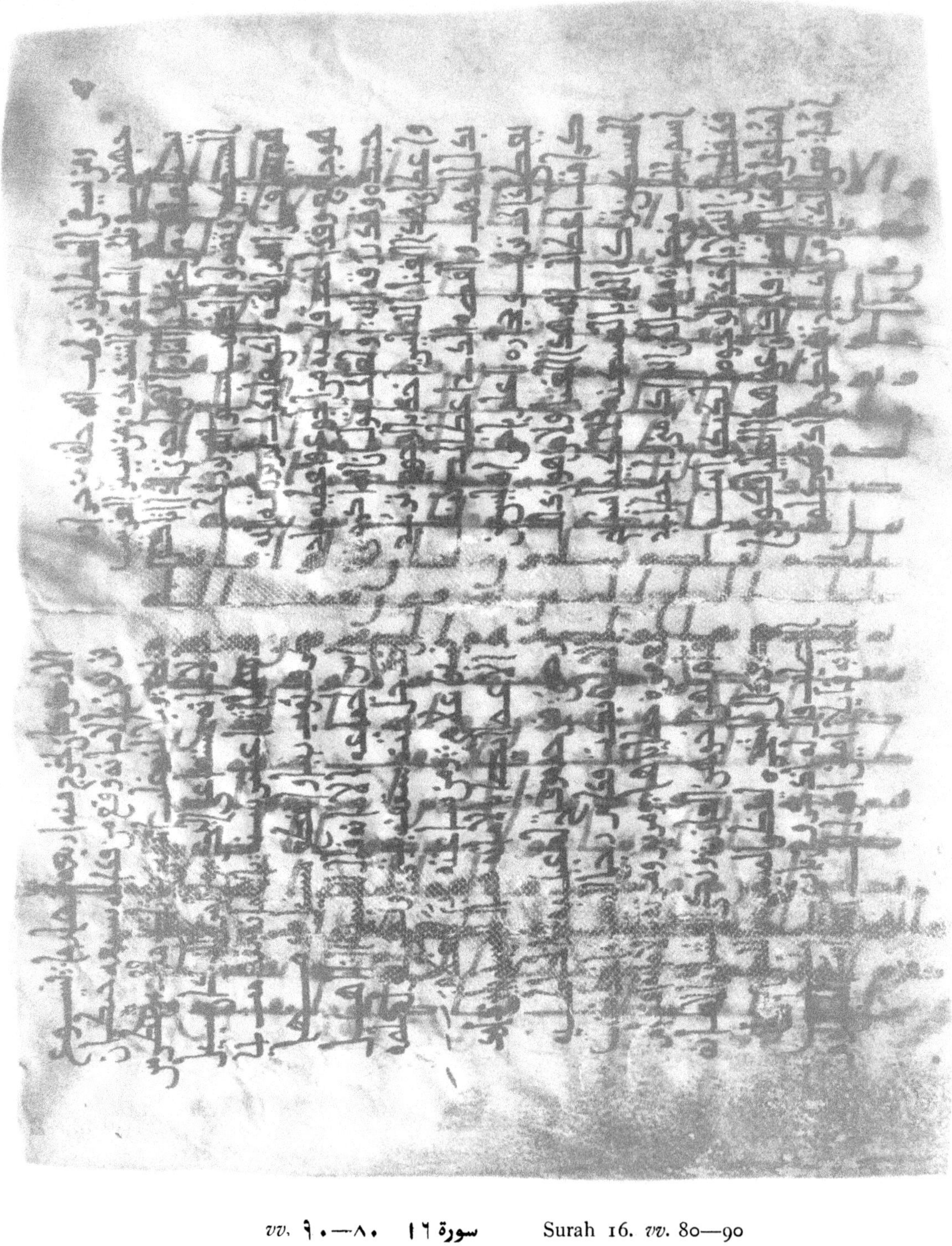

f. 55 a

سورة ١٦ ٨٠—٩٠ .vv   Surah 16. *vv.* 80—90

سورة ١٦

vv. ٨٠-٨١ والأفئدة لعلّكم تشكرون ألم يروا إلى الطّير
مسخّرات في جوّ السّمآء ما يمسكهنّ إلّا اللّه
v. ٨٢ إنّ في ذلك لآيات لقوم يؤمنون واللّه
جعل لكم من بيوتكم سكنا وجعل لكم من
جلود الأنعام بيوتا تستخفّونها يوم ظعنكم
ويوم إقامتكم ومن أصوافها وأوبارها
v. ٨٣ وأشعارها أثاثا ومتاعا إلى حين واللّه جعل
لكم ممّا خلق ظلالا وجعل لكم من الجبال
أكنانا وجعل لكم سرابيل تقيكم الحرّ وسرابيل
تقيكم بأسكم كذلك يتمّ نعمته
v. ٨٤ عليكم لعلّكم تسلمون فإن تولّوا فإنّما
v. ٨٥ عليك البلاغ المبين يعرفون نعمة اللّه
v. ٨٦ ثمّ ينكرونها وأكثرهم الكافرون ويوم
نبعث من كلّ أمّة شهيدا ثمّ لا يؤذن للّذين
v. ٨٧ كفروا ولا هم يستعتبون وإذا رأى الّذين
ظلموا العذاب فلا يخفّف عنهم ولا
v. ٨٨ هم ينظرون وإذا رأى الّذين أشركوا
شركآءهم قالوا ربّنا هؤلآء شركآؤنا الّذين كنّا
ندعو من دونك فألقوا إليهم القول إنّكم لكاذبون
v. ٨٩ وألقوا إلى اللّه يومئذ السّلم وضلّ عنهم ما كانوا يفترون
v. ٩٠ ألّذين كفروا وصدّوا عن سبيل اللّه زدناهم عذابا
فوق العذاب بما كانوا يفسدون

Fol. 58 a

سورة ١٦

v. 91 ويوم نبعث في كل امة شه[ي]دا عليهم من ا
نفسهم وجينا بك شهيدا على هولا ونزلنا
عليك الكتب تبينا لكل شاي وهدى
v. 92 ورحمة وبشرى للمسلمين. ان الله يامر بالعد
ل والاحسن واتا ذي القربى وينهى عن ا
لفحشا والمنكر والبغي يعظكم لعلكم تذ
v. 93 كرون. واوفوا بعهد الله اذا عهدتم
ولا تنقضوا الايمن بعد توكيدها وقد
جعلتم الله عليكم كفيلا ان الله يعلم
v. 94 ما تفعلون. ولا تكونوا كالتي نقضت
غزلها من بعد قوة انكثا تتخذون ايمنكم
دخلا بينكم ان تكون امة هي اربا (!) من ا Fol. 55 b
مة انما يبلوكم الله به وليبينن لكم يوم
v. 95 القيمة ما كنتم فيه تختلفون. ولو شا ا
لله جعلكم امة وحدة ولكن يضل الله
من يشا ويهدي من يشا ولتسلن عما كنتم
v. 96 تعملون. ولا تتخذوا ايمنكم دخلا
بينكم فتزل قدم بعد ثبوتها وتذوقو
ا السو بما صددتم عن سبيل الله ولكم
v. 97 عذاب عظيم. ولا تشتروا بعهد الله
ثمنا قليلا انما عند الله هو خير لكم
v. 98 ان كنتم تعلمون. ما عندكم ينفد وما

سورة ١٦

v. ٩١ ويوم نبعث في كلّ أمّة شهيدا عليهم من
أنفسهم وجئنا بك شهيدا على هؤلآء ونزّلنا
عليك الكتاب تبيانا لكلّ شيء وهدى
v. ٩٢ ورحمة وبشرى للمسلمين إنّ اللّه يأمر بالعدل
والإحسان وإيتآء ذي القربى وينهى عن
الفحشآء والمنكر والبغي يعظكم لعلّكم
v. ٩٣ تذكّرون وأوفوا بعهد اللّه إذا عاهدتم
ولا تنقضوا الأيمان بعد توكيدها وقد
جعلتم اللّه عليكم كفيلا إنّ اللّه يعلم
v. ٩٤ ما تفعلون ولا تكونوا كالّتي نقضت
غزلها من بعد قوّة أنكاثا تتّخذون أيمانكم
دخلا بينكم أن تكون أمّة هي أربى من
أمّة إنّما يبلوكم اللّه به وليبيّننّ لكم يوم
v. ٩٥ القيامة ما كنتم فيه تختلفون ولو شآء
اللّه لجعلكم أمّة واحدة ولكن يضلّ
من يشآء ويهدي من يشآء ولتسألنّ عمّا كنتم
v. ٩٦ تعملون ولا تتّخذوا أيمانكم دخلا
بينكم فتزلّ قدم بعد ثبوتها وتذوقوا
السّوء بما صددتم عن سبيل اللّه ولكم
v. ٩٧ عذاب عظيم ولا تشتروا بعهد اللّه
ثمنا قليلا إنّما عند اللّه هو خير لكم
v. ٩٨ إن كنتم تعلمون ما عندكم ينفد وما

Fol. 56b

سورة ١٦

v. 98 عند الله باق ولنجز[ين] الذين صبروا اجرهم
v. 99 باحسن ما كانوا يعملون. من عمل صلحا من ذ
كر او انثى وهو مومن ⟦لنحيينه⟧ (?) حيوة طيبة ولنجز
v. 100 ⟦يهم⟧ (?) اجرهم باحسن ما كانوا يعملون. فاذا
قرات القران فاستعذ بالله من
v. 101 الشيطن الرجيم. انه ليس له سلطن على الذ
v. 102 [ين امنوا وعلى] ربهم يتوكلون. انما
سلطنه على الذين يتولونه والذين هم
v. 103 به مشركون. واذا بدلنا اية مكان اية
والله اعلم بما ينزل قلوا انما انت
v. 104 مفتر بل اك[ثرهم] لا يعلمون. قل نزله رو
ح القدس من ربك بالحق ليثبت الذ — Fol. 57a
v. 105 ين امنوا وهدى وبشرى للمسلمين. ولقد
نعلم انهم يقولون انما يعلمه بشر لسن ا
لذي يلحدون اليه اعجمي وهذا لسن عربي
v. 106 مبين. ان الذين لا يومنون بايت الله
لا يهديهم الله ولهم عذاب اليم.
v. 107 انما يفتري الكذب الذين لا يومنون
بايت الله واوليك هم الكذبون.
v. 108 من كفر بالله من بعد ايمنه الا من اكره
وقلبه مطمن بالايمن ولكن من شرح با
لكفر صدرا فعليهم غضب من الله

سورة ١٦

v. ٩٨ عند اللّه باق ولنجزينّ الّذين صبروا أجرهم
v. ٩٩ بأحسن ما كانوا يعملون من عمل صالحا من
ذكر أو أنثى وهو مؤمن فلنحيينّه حيوة طيّبة ولنجزينّهم
v. ١٠٠ أجرهم بأحسن ما كانوا يعملون فإذا
قرأت القرآن فاستعذ باللّه من
v. ١٠١ الشّيطان الرّجيم إنّه ليس له سلطان على الّذين
v. ١٠٢ آمنوا وعلى ربّهم يتوكّلون إنّما
سلطانه على الّذين يتولّونه والّذين هم
v. ١٠٣ به مشركون وإذا بدّلنا آية مكان آية
واللّه أعلم بما ينزّل قالوا إنّما أنت
v. ١٠٤ مفتر بل أكثرهم لا يعلمون قل نزّله روح
القدس من ربّك بالحقّ ليثبّت الّذين
v. ١٠٥ آمنوا وهدى وبشرى للمسلمين ولقد
نعلم أنّهم يقولون إنّما يعلّمه بشر لسان
الّذي يلحدون إليه أعجميّ وهذا لسان عربيّ
v. ١٠٦ مبين إنّ الّذين لا يؤمنون بآيات اللّٰه
لا يهديهم اللّه ولهم عذاب أليم
v. ١٠٧ إنّما يفتري الكذب الّذين لا يؤمنون
بآيات اللّه وأولآئك هم الكاذبون
v. ١٠٨ من كفر باللّه من بعد إيمانه إلّا من أُكره
وقلبه مطمئنّ بالإيمان ولكن من شرح
بالكفر صدرا فعليهم غضب من اللّه

Fol. 56 a

سورة ١٦

vv. 108–9 ولهم عذاب عظيم. ذلك بانهم استحبو
ا الحيوة الدنيا على الاخرة وان الله لا
v. 110 يهدي القوم الكفرين. اوليك الذين طبع
الله على قلوبهم و[سمعهم وابصارهم واو]
ليك هم الغفلون لا جرم انهم في الاخرة
v. 111 هم الخسرون. ثم ان ربك للذين هجروا من
بعد ما فتنوا ثم جهدوا و[صبروا ان ربك]
v. 112 من بعدها لغفور رحيم. يوم تاتي كل نفس
تجدل عن نفسها وتوفى كل نفس ما عملته
v. 113 وهم لا يظلمون. وضرب الله مثلا قر
[ية] كانت امنة مط[مئنة ياتيها رزقها رغدا]
من كل مكان فكفرت بانعم الله فاذ Fol. 57 b
قها الله لبس [[الجوع والخوف بما كا]] ?
v. 114 نوا يصنعون. ولقد جاهم رسول من[هم فك]ذ
v. 115 بوه فاخذهم العذاب وهم ظلمون. فكلو
ا مما رزقكم الله حللا طيبا واشكروا
v. 116 نعمة الله ان كنتم ايه تعبدون. انما حرم
عليكم الميتة والدم ولحم [الخنزير] وما ا
هل لغير الله به فمن اضطر غير باغ ولا
v. 117 عاد فان الله غفور رحيم. ولا تقولوا لما

. . . .

حرام لتفتروا على الله الكذب ان الذين

سورة ١٦

٨-٩ ١٠ .vv ولهم عذاب عظيم ذلك بأنّهم استحبّوا
الحيوة الدّنيا على الآخرة وأنّ اللّه لا
١١٠ .v يهدي القوم الكافرين أولآئك الّذين طبع
اللّه على قلوبهم وسمعهم وأبصارهم وأولآئك
هم الغافلون لا جرم أنّهم في الآخرة
١١١ .v هم الخاسرون ثمّ إنّ ربّك للّذين هاجروا من
بعد ما فتنوا ثمّ جاهدوا وصبروا إنّ ربّك
١١٢ .v من بعدها لغفور رحيم يوم تأتي كلّ نفس
تجادل عن نفسها وتوفّى كلّ نفس ما عملت
١١٣ .v وهم لا يظلمون وضرب اللّه مثلا قرية
كانت آمنة مطمئنّة يأتيها رزقها رغدا
من كلّ مكان فكفرت بأنعم اللّه فأذاقها
اللّه لباس الجوع والخوف بما كانوا
١١٤ .v يصنعون ولقد جآءهم رسول منهم فكذّبوه
١١٥ .v فأخذهم العذاب وهم ظالمون فكلوا
ممّا رزقكم اللّه حلالا طيّبا واشكروا
١١٦ .v نعمة اللّه إن كنتم إيّاه تعبدون إنّما حرّم
عليكم الميتة والدّم ولحم الخنزير وما
أهلّ لغير اللّه به فمن اضطرّ غير باغ ولا
١١٧ .v عاد فإنّ اللّه غفور رحيم ولا تقولوا لما
تصف ألسنتكم الكذب هذا حلال وهذا
حرام لتفتروا على اللّه الكذب إنّ الّذين

Fol. 101 a

سورة ١٦

vv. 117–8 يفترون على الله الكذب لا يفلحون. متع
v. 119 قليل ولهم عذاب اليم. وعلى الذين هد
وا حرمنا ما قصصنا عليك من قبل وما ظلمنهم
v. 120 ولكن كانوا انفسهم يظلمون. ثم ان ربك
للذين عملوا السو بجهلة ثم تابوا من بعد ذ
لك واصلحوا ان ربك من بعدها لغفور
v. 121 رحيم. ان ابرهيم كان امة قنتا لله حنيفا
v. 122 ولم يك من المشركين. شكرا لانعمه ا
v. 123 جتبه وهديه الى صراط مستقيم. واتينه
[في الدنيا] حسنة وانه في الاخرة لمن الصلحين
v. 124 [ثم اوحينا اليك] ان اتبع ملة ابرهم(!) . .

Fol. 96 b . . . .

v. 125 على الذين اختلفوا [فيه] وان ربك ليحكم
بينهم يوم القيمة فيما كانوا فيه يختلفون
v. 126 ادع الى سبيل ربك بالحكمة وا
لموعظة الحسنة وجدلهم بالتي هي احسن
ان ربك هو اعلم بمن ضل عن سبيله وهو
v. 127 اعلم بالمهتدين. وان عقبتم فعقبوا بمثل
ما عوقبتم به ولين صبرتم لهو خير للصبرين
v. 128 واصبر وما صبرك الا بالله ولا تحزن
عليهم ولا تك في ضيق مما يمكرون
ان الله مع الذين اتقوا والذين هم محسنون

سورة ١٦

vv. ١١٧-٨ يفترون على اللّه الكذب لا يفلحون. متاع
v. ١١٩ قليل ولهم عذاب أليم وعلى الّذين هادوا
حرّمنا ما قصصنا عليك من قبل وما ظلمناهم
v. ١٢٠ ولكن كانوا أنفسهم يظلمون ثمّ إنّ ربّك
للّذين عملوا السّوء بجهالة ثمّ تابوا من بعد
ذلك وأصلحوا إنّ ربّك من بعدها لغفور
v. ١٢١ رحيم إنّ إبرهيم كان أمّة قانتا للّه حنيفا
v. ١٢٢ ولم يك من المشركين شاكرا لأنعمه
v. ١٢٣ إجتباه وهداه إلى صراط مستقيم وآتيناه
في الدّنيا حسنة وإنّه في الآخرة لمن الصّالحين
v. ١٢٤ ثمّ أوحينا إليك أن اتّبع ملّة إبرهيم
v. ١٢٥ حنيفا وما كان من المشركين إنّما جعل السّبت
على الّذين اختلفوا فيه وإنّ ربّك ليحكم
بينهم يوم القيامة فيما كانوا فيه يختلفون
v. ١٢٦ أدع إلى سبيل ربّك بالحكمة
والموعظة الحسنة وجادلهم بالّتي هي أحسن
إنّ ربّك هو أعلم بمن ضلّ عن سبيله وهو
v. ١٢٧ أعلم بالمهتدين وإن عاقبتم فعاقبوا بمثل
ما عوقبتم به ولئن صبرتم لهو خير للصّابرين
v. ١٢٨ واصبر وما صبرك إلّا باللّه ولا تحزن
عليهم ولا تك في ضيق ممّا يمكرون
إنّ اللّه مع الّذين اتّقوا والّذين هم محسنون

Fol. 101 b

سورة ١٧

v. 1 بسم الله الرحمن الرحيم سبحن الذي اسرى
بعبده ليلا من المسجد الحرم الى المسجد ا
لاقصى الذي بركنا حوله لنريه من ايتنا انه
v. 2 هو السميع البصير. واتينا موسى الكتب
وجعلنه هدى لبني اسريل الا تتخذوا من دوني
v. 3 وكيلا. ذرية من حملنا مع نوح انه كان عبد
v. 4 ا شكورا. وقضينا الى بني اسريل في الكتب
لتفسدن في الارض مرتين ولتعلن . . .
v. 5 . . . فاذا جا وعد اولا . . . .

Fol. 96 a . . . .

. . . وكان وعدا مف . . . .
v. 6 لكرة عليهم وامددنكم باموال وبنين و
v. 7 جعلنهم اكثر نفيرا. ان احسنتم احسنتم لا
نفسكم وان اساتم فلها فاذا جا وعد
الاخرة ليسوا وجوهكم وليدخلوا ا
لمسجد كما دخلوه اول مرة وليتبروا
v. 8 ما علوا تتبيرا. عسى ربكم ان يرحمكم
وان عدتم عدنا وجعلنا جهنم للكفرين
v. 9 حصيرا. ان هذا القران يهدي للتي هي اقو
v. 10 م [ويبشر] المومنين. الذين يعملون الصلحت

سورة ١٧

١ *v.* بسم اللّه الرّحمن الرّحيم سبحان الّذي أسرى
بعبده ليلا من المسجد الحرام إلى المسجد
الأقصى الّذي باركنا حوله لنريه من آياتنا إنّه
٢ *v.* هو السّميع البصير وآتينا موسى الكتاب
وجعلناه هدى لبني إسرآئل ألّا تتّخذوا من دوني
٣ *v.* وكيلا ذرّيّة من حملنا مع نوح إنّه كان عبدا
٤ *v.* شكورا وقضينا الى بني إسرآئل في الكتاب
لتفسدنّ في الأرض مرّتين ولتعلنّ علوّا كبيرا
٥ *v.* فإذا جآء وعد أولاهما بعثنا عليكم عبادا
لنا أولى بأس شديد فجاسوا خلال
٦ *v.* الدّيار وكان وعدا مفعولا ثمّ رددنا لكم
الكرّة عليهم وأمددناكم بأموال وبنين
٧ *v.* وجعلناكم أكثر نفيرا إن أحسنتم أحسنتم
لأنفسكم وإن أسأتم فلها فإذا جآء وعد
الآخرة ليسوؤا وجوهكم وليدخلوا
المسجد كما دخلوه أوّل مرّة وليتبّروا
٨ *v.* ما علوا تتبيرا عسى ربّكم أن يرحمكم
وإن عدتم عدنا وجعلنا جهنّم للكافرين
٩ *v.* حصيرا إنّ هذا القرآن يهدي للّتي هي أقوم
١٠ *v.* ويبشّر المؤمنين الّذين يعملون الصّالحات

Fol. 97 a

سورة ١٧

vv. 10–11 ان لهم اجرا كبيرا. وان الذين لا يومنون با
v. 12 لاخرة اع[تدنا لهم عذا]با اليما. ويدع
الانس[ان] بالشر دعاه بالخير وكان الانسن
v. 13 [عجولا]. وجعلنا الليل والنهر ايتين فمحونا
اية [الليل] وجعلنا اية النهر مبصرة لتبتغوا
فضلا من ربكم ولتعلموا عدد السنين وا
v. 14 [لحساب وكل] شاي فصلناه تفصيلا. وكل
انسن الزمنه طايره في عنقه ونخرج له يوم
v. 15 [ال]قيمة كتبا يلقه منشورا. اقرا كتبك
v. 16 كفى بنفسك اليوم عليك حسيبا. من اهتدى
[فانما يهتدي] لنفسه ومن ضل فا
Fol. 100 b [نما يضل عليها ولا] تزر وازرة وزر اخرى وما ك
v. 17 نا معذبين حتى نبعث رسولا. واذا اردنا
ان نهلك قرية امرنا مترفيها ففسقوا
فيها فحق عليها القول فدمرنها تدميرا.
v. 18 وكم اهلكنا من القرون من بعد نوح
وكفى بربك بذنوب عبده خبيرا
v. 19 بصيرا. من كان يريد العجلة عجلنا له فيها
ما نشا لمن نريد ثم جعلنا له جهنم يصليها
v. 20 مذموما مدحورا. ومن اراد الاخرة
وسعى لها سعيها وهو مومن فاوليك

سورة ١٧

vv. ١٠-١١ أنّ لهم أجرا كبيرا وأنّ الّذين لا يؤمنون
v. ١٢ بالآخرة أعتدنا لهم عذابا أليما ويدع
الإنسان بالشّرّ دعآءه بالخير وكان الإنسان
v. ١٣ عجولا وجعلنا اللّيل والنّهار آيتين فمحونا
آية اللّيل وجعلنا آية النّهار مبصرة لتبتغوا
فضلا من ربّكم ولتعلموا عدد السّنين
v. ١٤ والحساب وكلّ شيء فصّلناه تفصيلا وكلّ
إنسان ألزمناه طآئره في عنقه ونخرج له يوم
v. ١٥ القيامة كتابا يلقاه منشورا إقرأ كتابك
v. ١٦ كفى بنفسك اليوم عليك حسيبا من اهتدى
فإنّما يهتدي لنفسه ومن ضلّ فإنّما
يضلّ عليها ولا تزر وازرة وزر أخرى وما
v. ١٧ كنّا معذّبين حتّى نبعث رسولا وإذا أردنا
أن نهلك قرية أمرنا مترفيها ففسقوا
فيها فحقّ عليها القول فدمّرناها تدميرا
v. ١٨ وكم أهلكنا من القرون من بعد نوح
وكفى بربّك بذنوب عباده خبيرا
v. ١٩ بصيرا من كان يريد العاجلة عجّلنا له فيها
ما نشآء لمن نريد ثمّ جعلنا له جهنّم يصلاها
v. ٢٠ مذموما مدحورا ومن أراد الآخرة
وسعى لها سعيها وهو مؤمن فأولآئك

Fol. 97 b

سورة ١٧

vv. 20–21 كان سعيهم مشكورا. كلا نمد هولا و
هولا من عطا ربك وما كان عطا ر
v. 22 بك محظورا. انظر كيف فضلنا
بعضهم على بعض وللاخرة اكبر درجت
v. 23 واكبر تفضيلا. لا تجعل مع الله الها
v. 24 اخر فتقعد مذموما مخذولا. وقضى
ربك فلا تعبدوا الا اياه وبالولدين احسانا
اما يبلغن عندك الكبر احدهما او
كلهما فلا تقل لهما اف ولا تنهرهما
v. 25 وقل لهما قولا كريما. واخفض لهما جنا

Fol. 100a . . . .

. . . .

vv. 26–27 سكم ان تكونوا صلحين. فانه كان للاوابين
v. 28 غفورا. وات ذا القربى حقه والمسكين
v. 29 وابن السبيل ولا تبذر تبذيرا. ان المبذ
رين كانوا اخون الشيطين وكان الشيطن
v. 30 لربه كفورا. واما تعرضن عنهم ابتغا
رحمة من ربك ترجوها فقل لهم قولا ميسورا
v. 31 ولا تجعل يدك مغلولة الى عنقك ولا
تبسطها كل البسط فتقعد ملوما محسور
v. 32 ا. ان ربك يبسط الرزق لمن يشا ويقدر

سورة ١٧

vv. ٢٠-٢١ كان سعيهم مشكورا كلّا نمدّ هؤلآء
وهؤلآء من عطآء ربّك وما كان عطآء
v. ٢٢ ربّك محظورا أنظر كيف فضّلنا
بعضهم على بعض وللآخرة أكبر درجات
v. ٢٣ وأكبر تفضيلا لا تجعل مع اللّه إلها
v. ٢٤ آخر فتقعد مذموما مخذولا وقضى
ربّك ألّا تعبدوا إلّا إيّاه وبالوالدين إحسانا
إمّا يبلغنّ عندك الكبر أحدهما أو
كلاهما فلا تقل لهما أفّ ولا تنهرهما
v. ٢٥ وقل لهما قولا كريما واخفض لهما جناح
الذّلّ من الرّحمة وقل ربّ ارحمهما كما
v. ٢٦ ربّياني صغيرا ربّكم أعلم بما في نفوسكم
v. ٢٧ إن تكونوا صالحين فإنّه كان للأوّابين
v. ٢٨ غفورا وآت ذا القربى حقّه والمسكين
v. ٢٩ وابن السّبيل ولا تبذّر تبذيرا إنّ المبذّرين
كانوا إخوان الشّياطين وكان الشّيطان
v. ٣٠ لربّه كفورا وإمّا تعرضنّ عنهم ابتغآء
رحمة من ربّك ترجوها فقل لهم قولا ميسورا
v. ٣١ ولا تجعل يدك مغلولة إلى عنقك ولا
تبسطها كلّ البسط فتقعد ملوما محسورا
v. ٣٢ إنّ ربّك يبسط الرّزق لمن يشآء ويقدر

Fol. 98 a

سورة ١٧

vv. 32–33 انه كان بعبده خبيرا بصيرا. ولا تقتلوا
اولدكم خشية املق نحن نرزقهم وايكم
v. 34 ان قتلهم كان خطا كبيرا. ولا تقربوا [[الز
v. 35 نا]] (?) انه كان فحشة وسا سبيلا. ولا تقتلوا
النفس التي حرم الله الا بالحق ومن قتل
مظلوما [فقد] جعلنا لوليه سلطنا فلا يسر
v. 36 ف في القت[ل انه] كان منصورا. ولا تقر
بوا مل اليتيم الا بالتي هي احسن حتى يبلغ ا
شده واوفوا بالعهد ان العهد كان
v. 37 مسولا. واوفوا الكيل اذا كلتم وزنوا
. . . . . . ذلك خير وا . . . .
Fol. 99 b
v. 38 . . ولا . . . . . ليس لك به . . . . .
. . . .
v. 39 عنه مسولا. ولا تمش في الارض مرحا
انك لن تخرق الارض ولن تبلغ الجبل
v. 40 طولا. كل ذلك كان سية عند ر
v. 41 بك مكروها. ذلك مما اوحى ا
ليك ربك من الحكمة ولا تجعل مع الله
الها اخر فتلقى في جهنم ملوما مدحور
v. 42 ا. افاصفيكم ربكم بالبنين واتخذ
من المليكة انثا انكم لتقولون قولا

سورة ١٧

vv. ٣٢-٣٣ إنّه كان بعباده خبيرا بصيرا ولا تقتلوا
أولادكم خشية إملاق نحن نرزقهم وإيّاكم
v. ٣٤ إنّ قتلهم كان خطأ كبيرا ولا تقربوا الزّنا
v. ٣٥ إنّه كان فاحشة وسآء سبيلا ولا تقتلوا
النّفس الّتي حرّم اللّه إلّا بالحقّ ومن قتل
مظلوما فقد جعلنا لوليّه سلطانا فلا يسرف
v. ٣٦ في القتل إنّه كان منصورا ولا تقربوا
مال اليتيم إلّا بالّتي هي أحسن حتّى يبلغ
أشدّه وأوفوا بالعهد إنّ العهد كان
v. ٣٧ مسؤلا وأوفوا الكيل إذا كلتم وزنوا
بالقسطاس المستقيم ذلك خير وأحسن
v. ٣٨ تأويلا ولا تقف ما ليس لك به علم إنّ
السّمع والبصر والفؤاد كلّ أولآئك كان
v. ٣٩ عنه مسؤلا ولا تمش في الأرض مرحا
إنّك لن تخرق الأرض ولن تبلغ الجبال
v. ٤٠ طولا كلّ ذلك كان سيّئه عند
v. ٤١ ربّك مكروها ذلك ممّا أوحى
إليك ربّك من الحكمة ولا تجعل مع اللّه
إلها آخر فتلقى في جهنّم ملوما مدحورا
v. ٤٢ أفأصفاكم ربّكم بالبنين واتّخذ
من الملآئكة إناثا إنّكم لتقولون قولا

Fol. 98 b

سورة ١٧

vv. 42–43 عظيما. ولقد صرفنا في هذا القران ليذ
v. 44 كروا وما يزيدهم الا نفورا. قل لو
كان معه الهة كما يقولون اذا لابتغوا
v. 45 الى ذي العرش سبيلا. سبحنه وتعلى عما
v. 46 يقولون علوا كبيرا. تسبح له السمو
ت السبع والارض ومن [فيهن] وان من
شاي الا يسبح بحمده ولكن لا تفقهون
v. 47 تسبيحهم انه كان حليما غفورا. واذا
قرات القران جعلنا بينك وبين الذ
v. 48 ين لا يومنون بالاخرة حجابا مستورا. وجعلنا

Fol. 99 a . . . .

v. 49 . . . ا. واذا ذك[رت] ربك في [القران]
v. 50 وحده ولوا على ا[دبا]رهم نفورا. نحن
اعلم بما يستمعون به إذ يستمعون اليك
واذ هم نجوى اذ يقول الظلمون ان تتبعون
v. 51 الا رجلا مسحورا. انظر كيف ضربوا
لك الامثل فضلوا فلا يستطيعون سبيلا
v. 52 وقلوا ااذا كنا عظما ورفتا انا لمبعو
v. 53 ثون خلقا جديدا. قل كونوا حجرة او حد
يدا او خلقا مما يكبر في صدوركم
فسيقولون من يعيدنا قل الذي فطركم

سورة ١٧

vv. ٤٢-٤٣ عظيما ولقد صرّفنا في هذا القرآن
v. ٤٤ ليذّكّروا وما يزيدهم إلّا نفورا قل لو
كان معه آلهة كما يقولون إذا لابتغوا
v. ٤٥ إلى ذي العرش سبيلا سبحانه وتعالى عمّا
v. ٤٦ يقولون علوّا كبيرا تسبّح له السّموات
السّبع والأرض ومن فيهنّ وإن من
شيء إلّا يسبّح بحمده ولكن لا تفقهون
v. ٤٧ تسبيحهم إنّه كان حليما غفورا وإذا
قرأت القرآن جعلنا بينك وبين الّذين
v. ٤٨ لا يؤمنون بالآخرة حجابا مستورا وجعلنا
على قلوبهم أكنّة أن يفقهوه وفي آذانهم
v. ٤٩ وقرا وإذا ذكرت ربّك في القرآن
v. ٥٠ وحده ولّوا على أدبارهم نفورا نحن
أعلم بما يستمعون به إذ يستمعون إليك
وإذ هم نجوى إذ يقول الظّالمون إن تتّبعون
v. ٥١ إلّا رجلا مسحورا أنظر كيف ضربوا
لك الأمثال فضلّوا فلا يستطيعون سبيلا
v. ٥٢ وقالوا أئذا كنّا عظاما ورفاتا أئنّا لمبعوثون
v. ٥٣ خلقا جديدا قل كونوا حجارة أو حديدا
أو خلقا ممّا يكبر في صدوركم
فسيقولون من يعيدنا قل الّذي فطركم

Fol. 102b

سورة ١٧

v. 53 اول مرة فسينغضون اليك روسهم ويقو

v. 54 لون متى هو قل عسى ان يكون قريبا. يوم يد
عوكم فتستجيبون بحمده وتظنون ان لبثتم الا

v. 55 قليلا. وقل لعبدي يقولوا التي هي احسن
ان الشيطن ينزغ بينهم ان الشيطن كان للانسن

v. 56 عدوا مبينا. ربكم اعلم بكم ان يشا ير

. . . .

v. 57 . . . . اعلم بمن في السمو . .

(cætera legi non possunt)

سورة ١٧
v. ٥٣ أوّل مرّة فسينغضون إليك رؤسهم ويقولون
v. ٥٤ متى هو قل عسى أن يكون قريبا يوم
يدعوكم فتستجيبون بحمده وتظنّون إن لبثتم إلّا
v. ٥٥ قليلا وقل لعبادي يقولوا الّتي هي أحسن
إنّ الشّيطان ينزغ بينهم إن الشّيطان كان للإنسان
v. ٥٦ عدوّا مبينا ربّكم أعلم بكم إن يشأ
يرحمكم أو إن يشأ يعذّبكم وما أرسلناك
v. ٥٧ عليهم وكيلا وربّك أعلم بمن في السّموات
والأرض ولقد فضّلنا بعض النّبيّين على بعض
v. ٥٨ وآتينا داود زبورا قل ادعوا الّذين زعمتم
من دونه فلا يملكون كشف الضّرّ عنكم ولا
v. ٥٩ تحويلا أولآئك الّذين يدعون يبتغون إلى ربّهم
الوسيلة أيّهم أقرب ويرجون رحمته ويخافون
v. ٦٠ عذابه إنّ عذاب ربّك كان محذورا وإن
من قرية إلّا نحن مهلكوها قبل يوم القيامة
أو معذّبوها عذابا شديدا كان ذلك في الكتاب
v. ٦١ مسطورا وما منعنا أن نرسل بالآيات إلّا
أن كذّب بها الأوّلون وآتينا ثمود النّاقة
مبصرة فظلموا بها وما نرسل بالآيات

Fol. 158 b

سورة ٢٤

v. 17 . . . ويبين الله لكم ال . . .

v. 18 . . . كيم. ان الذين يحبون ان . . .

v. 19 . . . تشيع الفحشة في الذي . . .

v. 20 . . . وانتم لا تعلمون. ولولا . . .

. . . الله . . . روف رحيم . . .

v. 21 . . . خطوت الشيطن ومن يتبع خطو . . .

. . . والمنكر ولولا فض . . .

. . . منكم من احد ابدا ولكن الل . . .

v. 22 . . . ولا ياتل اولو الفضل

. . . القربى والمسكين والمه . . .

. . . وليصفحوا الا تحبون ان يغفر . . .

v. 23 . . . ان الذين يرمون المحصن . . .

. . . . Fol. 159a

v. 24 . . . تشهد عليهم السنتهم وايديهم . . .

v. 25 . . . يومئذ يوفيهم الله دينهم ا . . .

v. 26 . . . المبين. الخبيثت للخبيثين والخبيثون . . .

. . . للطيبين والطيبون للطيبت . . .

v. 27 . . . يقولون لهم مغفرة ورزق كريم. يا

. . . بيوتا غير بيوتكم حتى تستنسوا . . .

. . . ذلكم خير لكم لعلكم تذكرون . . .

v. 28 . . . فلا تدخلوها حتى يوذن لكم و . . .

. . . فارجعوا هو ازكى لكم والله . . .

v. 29 . . . عليكم جناح ان تدخلوا . . .

. . . لكم والله يعلم ما تبدون . .

سورة ٢٤
v. ١٧ ويبيّن اللّه لكم الآيات واللّه
v. ١٨ عليم حكيم إنّ الّذين يحبّون أن
v. ١٩ تشيع الفاحشة في الّذين آمنوا لهم عذاب أليم في الدّنيا
v. ٢٠ والآخرة واللّه يعلم وأنتم لا تعلمون ولولا
فضل اللّه عليكم ورحمته وأنّ اللّه رؤف رحيم
v. ٢١ يا أيّها الّذين آمنوا لا تتّبعوا خطوات الشّيطان ومن يتّبع
خطوات الشّيطان فإنّه يأمر بالفحشآء والمنكر ولولا فضل
اللّه عليكم ورحمته ما زكى منكم من أحد أبدا ولكنّ اللّه
v. ٢٢ يزكّي من يشآء واللّه سميع عليم ولا يأتل أولوا الفضل
منكم والسّعة أن يؤتوا أولي القربى والمساكين والمهاجرين
في سبيل اللّه وليعفوا وليصفحوا ألا تحبّون أن يغفر
v. ٢٣ اللّه لكم واللّه غفور رحيم إنّ الّذين يرمون المحصنات
الغافلات المؤمنات لعنوا في الدّنيا والآخرة ولهم عذاب عظيم
v. ٢٤ يوم تشهد عليهم ألسنتهم وأيديهم وأرجلهم
v. ٢٥ بما كانوا يعملون يومئذ يوفّيهم اللّه دينهم الحقّ
v. ٢٦ ويعلمون أنّ اللّه هو الحقّ المبين ألخبيثات للخبيثين والخبيثون
للخبيثات والطّيّبات للطّيّبين والطّيّبون للطّيّبات
v. ٢٧ أولآئك مبرّؤن ممّا يقولون لهم مغفرة ورزق كريم يا
أيّها الّذين آمنوا لا تدخلوا بيوتا غير بيوتكم حتّى تستأنسوا
وتسلّموا على أهلها ذلكم خير لكم لعلّكم تذكّرون
v. ٢٨ فإن لم تجدوا فيها أحدا فلا تدخلوها حتّى يؤذن لكم
وإن قيل لكم ارجعوا فارجعوا هو أزكى لكم واللّه
v. ٢٩ بما تعملون عليم ليس عليكم جناح أن تدخلوا
بيوتا غير مسكونة فيها متاع لكم واللّه يعلم ما تبدون

Fol. 161b

سورة ٢٨

v. 41 . . . وجعلنهم ايمة يدعون . . .

v. 42 . . . لا ينصرون. واتبعنهم في . . .

. . . يوم القيمة هم من المقبو . . .

v. 43 . . . الكتب من بعد ما ا . . .

. . . بصير للناس وهدى و . . .

v. 44 . . . كرون. وما كنت بجن . . .

. . . موسى الامر وما كنت من . . .

v. 45 . . . قرونا فتطول عليهم ا . . .

. . . ويا في اهل مدين تتلوا عليهم . . .

v. 46 . . . سلين. وما كنت بجنب ا . . .

. . . ولكن رحمة من ربك لتنذر . . .

. . . من قبلك لعلهم ية . . .

v. 47 . . . هم مصيبة بما قدمت ا . . . Fol. 156a

. . . لولا ارسلت الينا رسو . . .

v. 48 . . . ون من المومنين. فلما جاهم . . .

. . . اولم يكفروا بما اوتي . . .

. . . سحرن تظهرا وقالوا انا . . .

v. 49 . . . قل فاتوا بكتب من عند الله هو . . .

v. 50 . . . اتبعه ان كنتم صدقين. فان . . .

. . . علم انما يتبعون اهواهم . . .

. . . هواه بغير هدى من الله ان . . .

v. 51 . . . يهدي القوم الظلمين. ولقد وص . . .

. . . ول لعلهم يتذكرون . . .

سورة ٢٨
٤١ .v وجعلناهم أئمّة يدعون إلى النّار ويوم القيامة
٤٢ .v لا ينصرون وأتبعناهم في هذه الدّنيا لعنة
٤٣ .v ويوم القيامة هم من المقبوحين ولقد آتينا موسى
الكتاب من بعد ما أهلكنا القرون الأولى
بصآئر للنّاس وهدى ورحمة لعلّهم
٤٤ .v يتذكّرون وما كنت بجانب الغربيّ إذ قضينا إلى
٤٥ .v موسى الأمر وما كنت من الشّاهدين ولكنّا أنشأنا
قرونا فتطاول عليهم العمر وما كنت
ثاويا في أهل مدين تتلو عليهم آياتنا ولكنّا كنّا
٤٦ .v مرسلين وما كنت بجانب الطّور إذ نادينا
ولكن رحمة من ربّك لتنذر قوما ما أتاهم من نذير
٤٧ .v من قبلك لعلّهم يتذكّرون ولولا أن تصيبهم
مصيبة بما قدّمت أيديهم فيقولوا ربّنا
لولا أرسلت إلينا رسولا فنتّبع آياتك ونكون
٤٨ .v من المؤمنين فلمّا جآءهم الحقّ من
عندنا قالوا لولا أوتي مثل ما أوتي موسى
أولم يكفروا بما أوتي موسى من قبل قالوا
سحران تظاهرا وقالوا إنّا بكلّ كافرون
٤٩ .v قل فأتوا بكتاب من عند الله هو أهدى منهما
٥٠ .v أتّبعه إن كنتم صادقين فإن لم يستجيبوا لك
فاعلم أنّما يتّبعون أهوآءهم ومن أضلّ ممّن اتّبع
هواه بغير هدى من الله إنّ الله لا
٥١ .v يهدي القوم الظّالمين ولقد وصّلنا لهم
القول لعلّهم يتذكّرون

Fol. 160 a

سورة ٢٩

v. 17 . . . سول الا البلغ المبين . . .
v. 18 لله الخلق ثم يعيده ان ذا . . .
v. 19 يسير. قل سيروا في الارض . . .
بدا الخلق ثم الله ينشي ا . . .
v. 20 على كل شاي قدير. يعذب . . .
v. 21 واليه تقلبون. وما انتم بمعجزين . . .
لا في السما وما لكم من دون . . .
v. 22 نصير. والذين كفروا بايت . . .
يسوا من رحمتي واوليك لهم . . .
v. 23 كان جوب قومه الا ان قالوا اقتلوه . . .
فانجه الله من النار ان في ذلك . . .
v. 24 منون. قل انما اتخذتم من دون الله . . .
بينكم في الحيوة الدنيا ث . . .
بعضكم ببعض ويلعن بعضكم بع . . . Fol. 157 b
v. 25 النار وما لكم من نصرين. فامن له . . .
اني مهجر الى ربي انه هو العزيز الحكيم . . .
v. 26 له اسحق ويعقوب وجعلنا في ذريته . . .
والكتب واتينه اجره في الدنيا . . .
v. 27 ة لمن الصلحين. ولوطا اذ قل لقومه . . .
لتاتون الفحشة ما سبقكم بها . . .
v. 28 اينكم لتاتون الرجل وتقطعون . . .
تون في نديكم المنكر فما . . .
الا ان قالوا ايتنا . . .
v. 29 لصدقين. قل رب . . .
v. 30 لمفسدين. ولما جا . .

سورة ٢٩

vv. ١٧-١٨ الرسول إلّا البلاغ المبين أولم يروا كيف يبدئ
اللّه الخلق ثمّ يعيده إنّ ذلك على اللّه
v. ١٩ يسير قل سيروا في الأرض فانظروا كيف
بدأ الخلق ثمّ اللّه ينشئ النّشأة الآخرة إنّ اللّه
v. ٢٠ على كلّ شيء قدير يعذّب من يشآء ويرحم من يشآء
v. ٢١ وإليه تقلبون وما أنتم بمعجزين في الأرض
ولا في السّمآء وما لكم من دون اللّه من وليّ ولا
v. ٢٢ نصير والّذين كفروا بآيات اللّه ولقآئه أولآئك
v. ٢٣ يئسوا من رحمتي وأولآئك لهم عذاب أليم فما
كان جواب قومه إلّا أن قالوا اقتلوه أو حرّقوه
فأنجاه اللّه من النّار إنّ في ذلك لآيات لقوم
v. ٢٤ يؤمنون وقال إنّما اتّخذتم من دون اللّه أوثانا مودّة
بينكم في الحيوة الدّنيا ثمّ يوم القيامة يكفر
بعضكم ببعض ويلعن بعضكم بعضا ومأواكم
v. ٢٥ النّار وما لكم من ناصرين فآمن له لوط وقال
v. ٢٦ إنّي مهاجر إلى ربّي إنّه هو العزيز الحكيم ووهبنا
له إسحق ويعقوب وجعلنا في ذرّيّته النّبوّة
والكتاب وآتيناه أجره في الدنيا وإنّه في الآخرة
v. ٢٧ لمن الصّالحين ولوطا إذ قال لقومه إنّكم
لتأتون الفاحشة ما سبقكم بها من أحد من العالمين
v. ٢٨ أئنّكم لتأتون الرّجال وتقطعون السّبيل وتأتون
في ناديكم المنكر فما كان جواب قومه
إلّا أن قالوا ائتنا بعذاب اللّه إن كنت من
v. ٢٩ الصّادقين قال ربّ انصرني على القوم
v. ٣٠ المفسدين ولمّا جآءت

Fol. 152 a

سورة ٤٠

vv. 78–9 ن. الله الذي جعل لكم . . . . .

v. 80 ومنها تاكلون. ولكم فيها منافع ولتبلغوا [عليها]
حاجة في صدوركم وعليها وعلى ال[فلك]

vv. 81–2 تحملون. ويريكم ايته فاي ايت الله تنك[رون. ا]
فلم يسيروا في الارض فينظروا كيف [كان]
عقبة الذين من قبلهم كانوا اكثر منهم وا[شد]
قوة واثرا في الارض فما اغنى عنهم ما [كانوا]

v. 83 يكسبون. فلما جاتهم رسلهم بالبينت فر[حوا بما]
عندهم من العلم وحق بهم ما كانوا به يس[تهزؤن]

v. 84 فلما راوا باسنا قالوا امنا بالله وحده و[كفرنا]

v. 85 بما كنا به مشركين. فلم يكن نفعهم ايمنهم ل[ما راوا]
باسنا سنة الله التي قد خلت في عباده وخسر ه[نالك ا] Fol. 149 b
لكفرون

v. 1 بسم الله الرحمن الرحيم حم تنزيل من ا[لرحمن]

v. 2 الرحيم. كتاب فصلت ايته قرنا عربي[ا لقو]

v. 3 م يعلمون. بشيرا ونذيرا فاعرض اكثرهم [فهم لا]

v. 4 يسمعون. وقالوا قلوبنا في اكنة مما تدع[ونا اليه]
وفي اذنا وقر ومن بيننا وبينك حجاب فا[عمل ا]

v. 5 نما عملون. قل انما انا بشر مثلكم يوحا [الي انما]
الهكم اله واحد فاستقيموا اليه [واستغفروه]

v. 6 وويل للمشركين. الذين لا يوتون الزكوة . . .

f. 152a

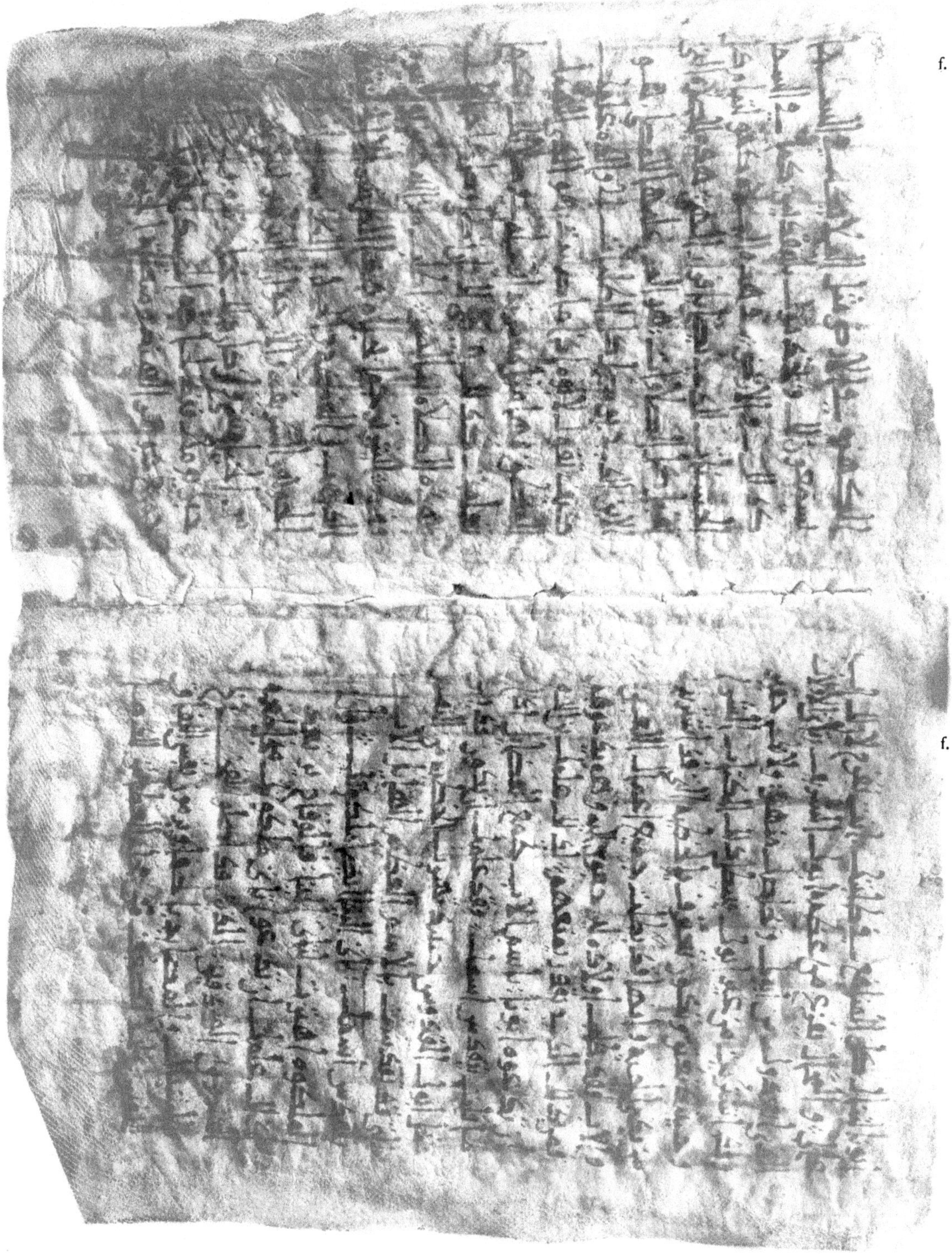

f. 149b

سورة ٤٠ v. ٧٨—سورة ٤١ v. ٦ Surah 40. v. 78—Surah 41. v. 6

سورة ٤٠

vv. ٧٨-٩ المبطلون. أللّه الّذي جعل لكم الأنعام لتركبوا منها
v. ٨٠ ومنها تأكلون ولكم فيها منافع ولتبلغوا عليها
حاجة في صدوركم وعليها وعلى الفلك
v. ٨١ تحملون ويريكم آياته فأيّ آيات اللّه تنكرون
v. ٨٢ أفلم يسيروا في الأرض فينظروا كيف كان عاقبة
الّذين من قبلهم كانوا أكثر منهم وأشدّ
قوّة وآثارا في الأرض فما أغنى عنهم ما كانوا
v. ٨٣ يكسبون فلمّا جآءتهم رسلهم بالبينات فرحوا بما
عندهم من العلم وحاق بهم ما كانوا به يستهزؤن
v. ٨٤ فلمّا رأوا بأسنا قالوا آمنّا باللّه وحده وكفرنا
v. ٨٥ بما كنّا به مشركين فلم يك ينفعهم إيمانهم لمّا رأوا
بأسنا سنّة اللّه الّتي قد خلت في عباده وخسر هنالك
الكافرون

سورة ٤١

v. ١ بسم اللّه الرّحمن الرّحيم حمّ تنزيل من الرّحمن
v. ٢ الرّحيم كتاب فصّلت آياته قرآنا عربيّا لقوم
v. ٣ يعلمون بشيرا ونذيرا فأعرض أكثرهم فهم لا
v. ٤ يسمعون وقالوا قلوبنا في أكنّة ممّا تدعونا إليه
وفي آذاننا وقر ومن بيننا وبينك حجاب فاعمل
v. ٥ إنّنا عاملون قل إنّما أنا بشر مثلكم يوحى إليّ أنّما
إلهكم إله واحد فاستقيموا إليه واستغفروه
v. ٦ وويل للمشركين الّذين لا يؤتون الزّكوة

Fol. 152b

سورة ۴۱

v. 9 . . . من فوقها و

. . . ها وقدر فيها اقوتها في اربعة ا[يام] سوا

v. 10 [للسائلين]. ثم استوى الى السما وهي دخن فقيل لها

[وللار]ض اتيا طوعا او كرها قلتا اتينا طايعين

v. 11 [فقضاه]ن سبع سموت في يومين واوحى في كل

[سمآء امر]ها وزينا السما الدنيا بمصبيح وحفظا

v. 12 [ذلك] تقدير العزيز العليم. فان اعرضوا فقل انذ

v. 13 [رتكم] صعقة مثل صعقة عاد وثمود. اذ جا

[تهم الر]سل من بين ايديهم ومن خلفهم الا تعبدوا

[الا الل]ه قالوا لو شا ربنا لانزل ملكة (!) فانا بما

v. 14 [ارسلتم] به كفرون. فاما عاد فاستكبروا في

[الارض] بغير الحق وقالوا من اشد منا قوة او . . . Fol. 149a

. . . لله الذي خلقهم هو اشد منهم قو . . .

v. 15 . . . ا باياتنا يجحدون. فارسلنا عليهم ريحا صر

[صرا في ا]يم نحست لنذيقهم عذاب الخزي في

[الحيوة ا]لدنيا ولعذاب الاخرة اخزى وهم لا

v. 16 [ينصرون]. واما ثمود فهدينهم فاستحبوا العمى

[على الهـ]ـدى فاخذتهم صعقة العذاب الهون

v. 17 [بما كانو]ا يكسبون. ونجينا الذين امنوا وكانوا يتقو

v. 18 [ن. ويوم يحشر] اعدا الله الى النار فهم يوزعون.

v. 19 [حتى اذا ما جاو]ها شهد عليهم سمعهم وابصرهم

v. 20 [وجلودهم بما كانوا يعملون]. وقالوا لجلودهم لم

سورة ۴١
v. ٩ وجعل فيها رواسي من فوقها
وبارك فيها وقدّر فيها أقواتها في أربعة أيّام سوآء
v. ١٠ للسّآئلين ثمّ استوى إلى السّمآء وهي دخان فقال لها
وللأرض ائتيا طوعا أو كرها قالتا أتينا طآئعين
v. ١١ فقضاهنّ سبع سموات في يومين وأوحى في كلّ
سمآء أمرها وزيّنّا السّمآء الدّنيا بمصابيح وحفظا
v. ١٢ ذلك تقدير العزيز العليم فإن أعرضوا فقل
v. ١٣ أنذرتكم صاعقة مثل صاعقة عاد وثمود إذ
جآءتهم الرّسل من بين أيديهم ومن خلفهم ألّا تعبدوا
إلّا اللّه قالوا لو شآء ربّنا لأنزل ملآئكة فإنّا بما
v. ١۴ أرسلتم به كافرون فأمّا عاد فاستكبروا في
الأرض بغير الحقّ وقالوا من أشدّ منّا قوّة أولم يروا
أنّ اللّه الّذي خلقهم هو أشدّ منهم قوّة
v. ١٥ وكانوا بآياتنا يجحدون فأرسلنا عليهم ريحا صرصرا
في أيّام نحسات لنذيقهم عذاب الخزي في
الحيوة الدّنيا ولعذاب الآخرة أخزى وهم لا
v. ١٦ ينصرون وأمّا ثمود فهديناهم فاستحبّوا العمى
على الهدى فأخذتهم صاعقة العذاب الهون
v. ١٧ بما كانوا يكسبون ونجّينا الّذين آمنوا وكانوا يتّقون
v. ١٨ ويوم يحشر أعدآء اللّه إلى النّار فهم يوزعون
v. ١٩ حتّى إذا ما جآؤها شهد عليهم سمعهم وأبصارهم
v. ٢٠ وجلودهم بما كانوا يعملون وقالوا لجلودهم لم

Fol. 151 a

سورة ٤٤

vv. 38–9 تو(!) الارض وما بينهما لعبين. ما خل[قنا]هما ا[لا بالحق

v. 40 ولكن اكثرهم لا يعلمون. ان يوملفصل(!) مي[قاتهم]

v. 41 اجمعين. يوم لا يغني مولى عن مولى شيا ولا هم ين[صرون]

vv. 42–3 الا من رحماللة(!) انه هو العزيز الرحيم. ان شجر[ة الزقو]

vv. 44–6 م. طعم الاثم. كالمهل يغلي في البطون. كغلي الحميم]

. . . .

. . . .

. . . .

. . . .

vv. 53–4 يلبسون من سندس واستبرق متقبلين. كذلك وز[وجناهم]

vv. 55–6 بحور عين. يدعون فيها بكل فكهة امنين. لا يذو[قون فيها]
الموت الا الموتة الاولى ووقاهم عذاب [الجحيم.]

vv. 57–8 فضلا من ربك ذلك هو الفوز العظيم. فانما[يسرناه] Fol. 150 b

v. 59 بلسنك لعلهم يتذكرون. فارتقب انهم م[رتقبون]

سورة ٤٥ بسم الله الرحمن الرحيم ٥ ٥ ٥ ٥ ٥ ٥

vv. 1–2 حم تنزيل الكتب من الله العزيز الحكيم. [ان في ا]

v. 3 لسموت والارض لايت للمومنين. وفي [خلقكم]

v. 4 وما يبث من دابة ايت [لقوم يو]قنون. واختلف [ال]
ليل والنهار وما انزل الله من السما من رزق فا[حيا به ا]
لارض بعد موتها وتصريف الريح ايت [لقوم]

v. 5 يعقلون. تلك ايت الله نتلوها عليك [بالحق]
فباي حديث بعد الله وا . . . .

سورة ٤٤

vv. ٣٨-٩ السّموات والأرض وما بينهما لاعبين ما خلقناهما إلّا بالحقّ

v. ٤٠ ولكنّ أكثرهم لا يعلمون إن يوم الفصل ميقاتهم

v. ٤١ أجمعين يوم لا يغني مولى عن مولى شيئا ولا هم ينصرون

vv. ٤٢-٣ إلّا من رحم الله إنّه هو العزيز الرّحيم إنّ شجرة الزّقّوم

vv. ٤٤-٦ طعام الأثيم كالمهل يغلي في البطون كغلي الحميم

vv. ٤٧-٨ خذوه فاعتلوه إلى سوآء الجحيم ثمّ صبّوا

v. ٤٩ فوق رأسه من عذاب الحميم ذق إنّك أنت

v. ٥٠ العزيز الكريم إنّ هذا ما كنتم به تمترون

vv. ٥١-٢ إنّ المتّقين في مقام أمين في جنّات وعيون

vv. ٥٣-٤ يلبسون من سندس وإستبرق متقابلين كذلك وزوّجناهم

vv. ٥٥-٦ بحور عين يدعون فيها بكلّ فاكهة آمنين لا يذوقون فيها
الموت إلّا الموتة الأولى ووقاهم عذاب الجحيم

vv. ٥٧-٨ فضلا من ربّك ذلك هو الفوز العظيم فإنّما يسّرناه

v. ٥٩ بلسانك لعلّهم يتذكّرون فارتقب إنّهم مرتقبون

سورة ٤٥ بسم الله الرّحمن الرّحيم

vv. ١-٢ حمٓ تنزيل الكتاب من الله العزيز الحكيم إنّ في

v. ٣ السّموات والأرض لآيات للمؤمنين وفي خلقكم

v. ٤ وما يبثّ من دابّة آيات لقوم يوقنون واختلاف
اللّيل والنّهار وما أنزل الله من السّمآء من رزق فأحيا به
الأرض بعد موتها وتصريف الرّياح آيات لقوم

v. ٥ يعقلون تلك آيات الله نتلوها عليك بالحقّ
فبأيّ حديث بعد الله وآياته يؤمنون

Fol. 151 b

سورة ٤٥

v. 9 . . . وا من دون الله اوليا ولهم عذاب
v. 10 [عظيم. هذا ه]دى والذين كفروا بايت ربهم
v. 11 [لهم عذاب من] رجز اليم. الله الذي سخر لكم البحر
[لتجري ال]فلك فيه بامره ولتبتغوا من فضله ولعلكم
v. 12 [تش]كرون. وسخر لكم ما في السموت وما في الا
[رض] جميعا منه ان في ذلك لايت لقوم يتفك
v. 13 [رون]. قل للذين امنوا يغفروا للذين لا يرجون ايام ا
v. 14 [لله ليجز]ي قوما بما كانوا يكسبون. من عمل صلحا
[فلنف]سه ومن اسا فعليها ثم الى ربكم ترجعون.
v. 15 [ولقد] اتينا بني اسرايل الكتب والحكم والنبوة
[ورزقنا]هم من الطيبت وفضلنهم على العلمين. Fol. 150 a
v. 16 [وآ]تينهم بينت من الامر فما اختلفوا الا من بعد
[ما جاء]هم العلم بغيا بينهم ان ربك يقضي بينهم
v. 17 [يوم] القيمة فيما كانوا فيه يختلفون. ثم جعلنك
[على] شريعة من الامر فاتبعها ولا تتبع اهوا الذين
v. 18 [لا يعلم]ون. انهم لن يغنوا عنك من الل[[كم]] ؟ هكما
[وان الظال]مين بعضهم اوليا بعض والله ولي المتقين.
v. 19 [هذا بصا]ير للناس وهدى ورحمة لقوم يوقنون.
v. 20 [ام] حسب الذين اجترحوا السيت ان نجعلهم
[كالذين آمنوا] وعملوا الصلحت سوا محيهم

سورة ٤٥

٩ .v من دون اللّه أوليآء ولهم عذاب
١٠ .v عظيم هذا هدى والّذين كفروا بآيات ربّهم
١١ .v لهم عذاب من رجز أليم ألله الّذي سخّر لكم البحر
لتجري الفلك فيه بأمره ولتبتغوا من فضله ولعلّكم
١٢ .v تشكرون وسخّر لكم ما في السّموات وما في
الأرض جميعا منه إنّ في ذلك لآيات لقوم يتفكّرون
١٣ .v قل للّذين آمنوا يغفروا للّذين لا يرجون أيّام
١٤ .v اللّه ليجزي قوما بما كانوا يكسبون من عمل صالحا
فلنفسه ومن أسآء فعليها ثمّ إلى ربّكم ترجعون
١٥ .v ولقد آتينا بني إسرآئل الكتاب والحكم والنّبوّة
ورزقناهم من الطّيّبات وفضّلناهم على العالمين
١٦ .v وآتيناهم بيّنات من الأمر فما اختلفوا إلّا من بعد
ما جآءهم العلم بغيا بينهم إنّ ربّك يقضي بينهم
١٧ .v يوم القيامة فيما كانوا فيه يختلفون ثمّ جعلناك
على شريعة من الأمر فاتّبعها ولا تتّبع أهوآء الّذين
١٨ .v لا يعلمون إنّهم لن يغنوا عنك من اللّه شيئا
وإنّ الظّالمين بعضهم أوليآء بعض واللّه وليّ المتّقين
١٩ .v هذا بصآئر للنّاس وهدى ورحمة لقوم يوقنون
٢٠ .v أم حسب الّذين اجترحوا السّيّآت أن نجعلهم
كالّذين آمنوا وعملوا الصّالحات سوآء محياهم

Ingram Content Group UK Ltd.
Milton Keynes UK
UKHW051058310523
422617UK00024B/244

9 781107 438040